CYBERSECURITY
Is Everybody's
Business

Solve the Security Puzzle
for Your Small Business and Home

SCOTT N. SCHOBER

with Craig

D1510271

Cybersecurity Is Everybody's Business

Copyright © 2019 Scott N. Schober and Craig W. Schober

Published by ScottSchober.com Publishing
Metuchen, New Jersey

ISBN 978-0-9969022-5-0 (hardcover)
ISBN 978-0-9969022-6-7 (paperback)
ISBN 978-0-9969022-7-4 (e-book)

Cover & Interior Design by GKS Creative, Nashville
Illustrations by Jake Thomas of Jake Thomas Creative
Project Management by The Cadence Group

This book may be purchased for educational, business, or sales
promotional use. For information, please email info@scottschober.
com, 732-548-3737, or visit www.ScottSchober.com.

Contents

Introduction

"Stay safe." These simple parting words are how I ended my first book, *Hacked Again*, and also how I end every episode from my weekly *2 Minute CyberSecurity Briefing* video podcast. They resonate with me but sometimes more from fear than confidence. All the cybersecurity knowledge in the world cannot stop the indisputable fact that, at the end of the day, we are accountable only for our own actions. I can't begin to fathom what readers, listeners, viewers, friends, coworkers, and even loved ones take away from my advice and implement in their own security protocols. I would have to be a snooping hacker to know such details. I would also have to be a mind reader to ascertain why people who know my experiences, my business, and me personally don't take the next step to change their passwords or manually type in that URL rather than clicking on that email link, for instance.

Whenever I finish speaking to a cybersecurity group, share details from the latest cyberbreach with TV audiences, or post my latest blog to a never-ending march of social media agents, the only thing I am confident in is that I do *not* know what will happen next. Will they follow my advice? And why should they? After all, I'm the cybersecurity expert whose business was hacked. Are people taking me seriously? Well, the answer might surprise you as much as it has me over the past three years or so.

Since I began this journey of reading, writing, and speaking out on cybersecurity best practices, it has gone on to become an integral part of everyone's daily lives. Conversations around the proverbial watercooler have morphed from personal anecdotes into full-blown conversations about the Ashley Madison hack. From inconsequential jokes to conspiracy theories surrounding Russians hacking the US presidential elections. From talking about the weather to talking about the FBI and NSA invading our lives. These exchanges might not end with a clear call to action or even a "Stay safe," but they indicate the ever-growing reach of cybersecurity into our fears and hopes. Life on the internet is boundless with possibilities, while at the same time, it's bound by an increasing fear of those who would spy on us, hack us, and blackmail us and our loved ones.

Compromises of personal data have become so commonplace that cyber insurance is just another checkbox next to our car insurance. Colleges and universities offer both undergraduate and master's degrees in cybersecurity. Countless cybersecurity startups have popped up overnight with no shortage of investors eager to fund their efforts.

For me, not a day goes by without someone sharing a personal story of being victimized by a cyberthief. I suppose a title like *Hacked Again* would attract such a reader, but I wouldn't have believed it was so prevalent before I published my book. Their stories are all unique, but they all start on the same common ground. Perhaps the debit card they swiped at a seemingly benign parking garage or clicking on an email link from a once trusted e-commerce website. Whatever it was, all of their stories can be attributed more to muscle memory rather than a lack of judgment. And after being hacked, these victims all end up in a similar state of mind with a progression of truths and coping mechanisms. All of them find themselves somewhere in the midst of the five stages of hacking victims: ignorance, shock, reenactment, acknowledgment, and rectification.

Ignorance: You are carefree and thinking about anything but being hacked. Ignorance is never bliss in the world of cybersecurity.

Shock: What is going on? How could that money be debited from my account? Why is my computer crashing constantly? Someone is now demanding ransom to give my data back! The shock typically lasts just seconds but leaves that same pit in all victims' stomachs. It is similar to learning about the death of a loved one or receiving a huge blow to the ego.

Reenactment: How did this happen? Many hacking victims seamlessly fall out of shock and straight into backtracking the steps that led them to their current predicament. They all figure that if only they could reenact their security missteps, they might be able to somehow think their way out of this situation. Did I log into the wrong account? What computer did I last log into, and who could've been looking over my shoulder? More often than not, the answers are already staring them in the face, just waiting for them to finish going through the paces. You see, as soon as victims begin to recreate their steps, they also are recreating the crime. At that point, they are now acknowledging that they've been hacked, and there's no going back.

Acknowledgment: Three steps later and they have finally stepped into their role as a hacking victim. It's a hard pill for anyone to swallow. I'm an expert, and I had to swallow that giant horse pill myself when I was hacked. It goes down slowly. For some, it amounts to no more than a party conversation about their Facebook accounts being hijacked. The embarrassment has already subsided, so they can play it as a funny anecdote involving a weekend of obscene postings and rude comments on their page. Others are not so lucky.

Short of being a cybersecurity-forensics expert, most victims have no means of knowing whether they are or will ever be fully in the clear. Hackers can repurpose old content in an effort to create new hacks. That password you know you changed to shore up your online banking security wasn't used only once: You forgot that you briefly dabbled in eBay two years ago as a seller. Of course, you accepted payments through PayPal but did you remember that you also used that same old online banking password for your PayPal account? It's only a matter of time before the same hacker or one of their password buyers reminds you there is more than one point of entry to compromise your life's savings. But I'm jumping the gun here because we haven't even gotten to the final stage of hacking victims yet.

Rectification: Your online-banking hacker was all set to go through your website history to give your weak password a try all over the internet, but you've already rectified the damage by building up your defenses to prevent further hacks. Instead of simply acknowledging that you were hacked and then procrastinating yourself into inaction, you took steps. You immediately changed all of your passwords to stronger ones. You backed up all of your data. You went through all old emails to refresh your memory about past online transactions, correspondences, or registrations that could lead you into being hacked again.

You took a violation and turned it into a personal triumph. You exterminated every bug in your home and set up traps to catch any stragglers. You took cyberlemons and opened up an e-commerce lemonade stand. Sounds great, right? Unfortunately, my little motivational speech belies a hard truth in cybersecurity: very few people actually change their online habits.

Even after suffering from these stages of being hacked, most folks go through the first four stages but peter out at the last, most important stage. And the ones who haven't been hacked yet (or at least don't realize they've been hacked) have the best of intentions. These are the same people who retweet cybersecurity tips, sit through webinars, and have even paid good money for my book. What are they thinking when it comes to the part where they take control of their cyber defenses?

The first thing nearly every reader of *Hacked Again* tells me is that before they have even finished reading it, they've changed their least secure passwords into stronger ones. That's a great start, but according to the internet security teams at Symantec and Verizon, nearly one million new malware threats are released every single day.

These malware strains don't write themselves. There is a demand for skilled hackers, both ethical and black hat, but the black hats play by different rules. They buy and sell passwords, credit card numbers, and zero-day exploits (a security flaw with no known software patches) to the highest bidder. The job market for illegal hacking is growing as fast as the Dark Web itself, which means that all users must not only take steps but also continue practicing a cyber-safe lifestyle. It's no different than dieting. If your trainer has set a goal for you to lose ten pounds and keep it off, you won't reach it by avoiding carbs for only one day. Sure you can shave some pounds off by temporarily fasting and avoiding certain foods for a while, but in order to keep that weight off, you must incorporate those changes into your lifestyle. Cybersecurity best practices need to become standard practices for all internet users.

I cannot help but feel I haven't done enough myself and I haven't done enough to get the word out. Many tell me they're listening and have every intention to make security-minded changes, but incidents of ransomware, phishing, identity theft, and malware are all trending up with no letup in sight. We are all on a collision course with the darker parts of ourselves. As citizens of the internet, no one else can keep us safe from other less scrupulous individuals; that is every person's responsibility. As a cybersecurity expert, it's also my job to inform and educate as many of you as possible. After all, you don't have the time to research malware and educate others on the best way to avoid it. So here we are, and here I am with a new book!

To be honest, I considered many different book titles. For the past year, I've kept a list of dozens of potential titles. Some were flashy, and some were downright SEO friendly. But in my head, I kept coming back to a single phrase, which was even a chapter title in *Hacked Again*, and it speaks volumes to the state of cybersecurity and our collective role in this new, more dangerous world.

Cybersecurity Is Everybody's Business is part catch-up and part prognostication but is mostly about the here and now. The tech world has reached the point of no return. Since we cannot simply shut off or slow down any part of the internet, we must face it together. Some of us will lean more heavily on others, but we will all contribute to the greater cause of keeping technology safe for everyone. Some define "business" as a chore and some as an opportunity, but since we all live digitally connected lives, it's all of our business. For my part, I have dedicated years of research, education, and invention to help others lead safer digital lives. I advise anyone looking for fulfillment in the tech sector to educate themselves and share that knowledge with everyone else they meet. If I've inspired just one individual to do so, I've done my job and will continue to do so.

The only thing to do with good advice is to pass it on.
It is never of any use to oneself.
—Oscar Wilde (1854–1900)

In an effort to avoid covering the same old ground, I have kept the *Hacked Again* revisits to a minimum. Some of the major breaches and cybersecurity scandals that were covered in *Hacked Again* are still unfolding as smaller aftershocks, so I would be remiss in avoiding them entirely. After all, the best way to learn about cybersecurity is by avoiding the mistakes of others. The year 2016 was full of them. I was just finishing up *Hacked Again* at the tail end of 2015, so I wasn't able to address huge cybersecurity stories, such as Ashley Madison, Sony Pictures, and Apple's encryption fight with the FBI. Those stories set the stage and took us into the rest of 2016, a year full of gargantuan hacks both in size and importance.

We saw huge chunks of the internet, including Netflix, CNN, and Twitter, taken down by a massively orchestrated cyberattack. We also saw our US democracy compromised by Russian hackers who breached the Democratic National Committee (DNC) and the Democratic Congressional Campaign Committee (DCCC), only to turn over their data to WikiLeaks. Democracy and privacy took another hit when a white hat hacker uncovered a giant voter database containing the personal information of 191 million registered American voters sitting on the open web. In addition to those massive hacks, we also saw cars, drones, and all kinds of IoT, or the "internet of things," devices getting hacked. Health-care, tech companies, and banking institutions saw their share of breaches as well.

Since I've researched, made public speeches, and written about these issues in varying degrees over the past two years, I've been able to filter out the most meaningful questions and answers for you. After hearing the same softballs lobbed at me repeatedly, the best questions jump out and make me think. Many other experts are thinking, too, so when we pool our experiences, we have come up with some pretty good answers. The *who, what,* and *when* are never quite as interesting as the *why* and *how,* but all the questions and answers work together to help us protect ourselves and each other.

From the massive server hacks on Yahoo all the way down to your own personal computer, the same security principles apply, which is why I will take you through them all. Of course, no cybersecurity book would be complete without a deep dive into passwords—not just the theoretical but also the practical. I cover passwords in a way that challenges and entices readers to make cybersecurity changes for the better. And the same goes for other security topics, including social engineering, hacker psychology, and your digital footprints. Encryption, spam, phishing, and the latest malware scams will also be discussed at length.

In an effort to make the content even more accessible, I will be releasing a compendium of short videos that correspond to each section free to all of my readers. Sometimes pictures are better than words, and video is better than text. With enough mediums covered, I'm wagering that my words and advice won't simply fall by the wayside. I have to be willing to put in the time if I really want you to follow my advice completely. You can make a hacker's job easy by providing them with many points of attack, but I can twist that same principle to my advantage too. By creating multiple points of engagement—through text, video, social media, audiobooks, etc.—I will have amassed the greatest informed audience who is ready to take on any cybersecurity challenge ahead. And even if you don't read this book and have never heard of me, I'll still see you there. After all, *cybersecurity really is everybody's business.*

Part 1: Minding Your Own Business

CHAPTER 1

The "Cyber" in Cybersecurity

The word "cybersecurity" can give many people that glazed-over look, whether I am trying to explain the theoretical benefits of encryption or the hidden threats of malware. I like to think that it's the material and not my personality that turns them off, so I resort to using metaphors and anecdotes to keep the conversations lively. One of the most effective metaphors is old-fashioned door locks and home-security systems. After all, there is something about a

3

device we use every day and can get our hands on that easily lends itself to relevant discussion of the less tangible aspects of security—the "cyber" in cybersecurity.

In my first book, *Hacked Again*, I drew many connections to the importance of layers in both physical security and cybersecurity. Unless you live in one of those mythical small towns where everyone leaves their doors unlocked, you are already protecting your home with layers of security. So I want to spend a few pages of your time elaborating on physical security for your home so you can appreciate the importance of each layer and find its analogy for each layer of cybersecurity. It's important to remember that no single layer can be more effective than the sum of all the layers. This is because no one layer of security will stop the average thief, which is why we implement many layers. While only a truly determined thief will get through most or all of your defenses, 99 percent of them will give up before ever setting foot in your home. At the end of the day, it's just a numbers game, and nowhere is that more apparent than in cybersecurity.

Do you live in a single-family home or something more like an apartment or condominium complex? Many assume that large apartment complexes in large cities face considerably more security and safety issues due to the intensified criminal element among a larger population in a confined area. Well, they are both right and wrong in their assumptions, and it's mostly due to layers of security. While houses contain multiple attack vectors, such as street-level windows, back doors, garage doors, basement doors, etc., the homeowners also have more control over their security options, such as alarm systems, video cameras, warning signs, and even guard dogs.

Similarly, apartment dwellers have to deal with accessible fire escapes, unaccounted-for strangers slipping into their building, and copies of keys readily supplied by former tenants, in addition to landlords, superintendents, and anyone else in the mix. However, those inherent security weaknesses can be countered by multiple vestibule doors, multifloor layouts, and neighbor proximity for instant response to suspicious noises or activity.

My point is that there's no one foolproof way to secure your safety, privacy, and belongings. The only way to increase your security is by decreasing the likelihood of physical or network penetration by increasing the number of layers or security challenges.

WI-FI SECURITY

In the world of cybersecurity, your front door is akin to direct access to your Wi-Fi network. Readily available, free Wi-Fi hacking tools (Aircrack-ng, AirSnort, Wireshark, etc.) allow cyberthieves to gain entry the same way a locksmith gains entry: through your locked door. These hacking tools are not criminal by nature; they are used by both sides of the law (meaning both black and white hats) and anyone interested in security weaknesses by sniffing packets, detecting drivers, and identifying known manufacturer vulnerabilities. These software programs are also often command-line friendly, allowing for heavy scripting and customization. This is where users begin to choose a side. Security researchers and even penetration testers might require and use customizable tools, but they have a very different endgame than the criminals.

Wi-Fi is exceptionally easy to compromise when left open without any default security standard in place. Many manufacturers of cheaper wireless devices still do not require a security standard to be selected by the user, so users are led down an insecure path right from the start. When users actually select a wireless application protocol, such as WPA2—which is much more secure than wired equivalent privacy (WEP) and WPA because it requires stronger encryption—they must create a long, strong password to ensure that hackers cannot easily guess or quickly brute force their way into the network. But when users lazily write down those same passwords and stick them under a Wi-Fi router, they have completely undermined their own cybersecurity. It can theoretically take supercomputers millions of years to brute-force attack a Wi-Fi password by using Advanced Encryption Standard (AES) in WPA2, but with physical access, a hacker has reduced millions of years to just seconds.

Manufacturers of inexpensive network products also allow users to fully configure their Wi-Fi devices without even changing the default service set identifier (SSID) or name. By allowing users to keep the default username—and sometimes the default password too—anyone can easily identify the brand and find its associated exploits. This is much like listing your home in the yellow pages under the category of "Homes with Unlocked Front Doors." Besides changing your service set identifier (SSID), you can also opt not to broadcast it, which I recommend. You can even require your Wi-Fi users to type in the network name with exact spelling before they can even see and connect to it. Not all routers support this feature so be sure to do a little research before buying or a little research on your existing router to benefit from true wireless anonymity. These are the basic steps:

1. Launch your router's web-based setup page or its included PC software.

2. Go to the WIRELESS tab to edit your wireless settings.

3. Disable the SSID Broadcast.

Note: When SSID Broadcast is disabled and someone you trust wants to utilize your Wi-Fi network as a guest, you will need to give them your SSID name and guest password.

BRUTE FORCE IS EFFECTIVE

One of the simplest things that any computer user can do to secure their computer is to require a strong password to wake up their PC or mobile devices. There are many techniques to gain entry, but they all come back to the password. These passwords are like the tumblers inside a door lock.

The American National Standards Institute (ANSI) has developed an excellent standard for three different grades of door locks:

- Lock grade 3 meets residential building requirements but provides only minimal security. It can withstand 200,000 cycles, two door strikes, and a 150-pound weight test.

- Lock grade 2 locks double those numbers.
- Lock grade 1 triples them.

Your door's lock grade might not be visible, but in the world of locks, ruggedness can be likened to length and complexity of passwords.

I want to remind readers that new security technologies, particularly the unvetted ones, bring about their own set of unique problems. Smart locks have become a hot item in the world of home automation and security. There are several offerings currently on the market, with new ones popping up all the time from first-time vendors. A smart lock is any lock that ties into your home's digital network and/or can be controlled by an app or some automation software. Most use Bluetooth, Wi-Fi, or Z-Wave wireless standards to communicate with the hardware portion of the lock. Unfortunately, smart locks are susceptible to not only physical brute force attacks but also software hacks.

In 2016 Tapplock raised over $320,000 on Kickstarter, but since raising the funds and releasing its product, the company has had nothing but problems. In his review of Tapplock for Pen Test Partners, Andrew Tierney managed to crack the security of his lock and write an Android app that would also crack any other Tapplock installed as well.[1] After giving Tapplock a week to respond to his claims before going public, the company simply sent an alert to its customers that all Tapplocks required a new firmware update in

---

1   Thomas Brewster, "Tapplock: This $100 'Smart Lock' Can Be Hacked Open In 2 Seconds," *Forbes*, June 13, 2018, https://www.forbes.com/sites/thomasbrewster/2018/06/13/tapplock-smart-lock-hacked-in-2-seconds/#407af4771333.

order to be secure. The vulnerability was a product of the Bluetooth communication protocols, but that was not the only weakness. Another security researcher found flaws in the account creation setup, allowing every Tapplock to be opened by anyone. In addition to those digital security flaws, the claimed "unbreakable durability" in the hardware was composed of a poor aluminum alloy found to be brittle, weak, and not very resistant to high temperatures. And finally, the back of the lock itself could be readily unscrewed and removed by a common screwdriver. Tapplock just goes to show that even security-focused high-tech products can be their own worst enemies, so never jump into an unproven security solution headfirst.

Burglaries happen every thirteen seconds on average in the United States, and approximately 33 percent of them involve a forced entry through the front door. Thieves know they can kick through the majority of doors with relative ease and minimal noise. In the movies, thieves pick locks in seconds, but it takes longer in the real world, and no criminal wants to be so conspicuous for that long. Brute force does the job in the real world and can be even more effective in the cyberworld.

Remember the iCloud celebrity account hacks? That was a direct result of brute-force attacks that exploited Apple's failure to implement more robust security layers. More recently, a company called Grayshift released a box called GrayKey. This box has been purchased by law-enforcement agencies across the United States for the simple task of hacking criminal suspects' iPhones. The device claims to exploit iPhones running the latest Apple iOS software (versions up to 11.3 as of this writing) by brute forcing four- or six-digit numeric passcodes at an extremely high rate. This is accomplished only by taking advantage of a security weakness discovered in iOS and making thousands of random passcodes per second.

- A basic four-digit code takes minutes to crack.
- A six-digit code takes a little over ten hours for this box to crack.
- An eight-digit code will generally take a little more than a month.
- A ten-digit passcode will take between 150 and 300 months to hack.
- Simply add some special characters in your ten-digit code, and that phone will take up to twenty-five years to hack!

My point is that, at the end of the day, even if your front door lock has hundreds of tumblers, making it nearly impossible for experts to pick, it doesn't matter if any thief can simply kick it in.

And speaking of front-door durability, most bolt lock plates utilize one-half-inch screws, and the same holds true for most door hinges. You can easily replace these default screws with longer three-inch screws available from any hardware store, like I did. This substantially prevents the possibility of any successful brute force attacks on your door—another simple layer of security that may be invisible to most thieves but still provides peace of mind to homeowners.

This upgrade in the chain of security can be compared to your password keychain on computers. Both Apple and Microsoft offer encrypted password protection across devices on their hardware platforms, as does Google, which offers similar protections in its Chrome browser. These offerings lean a little more toward convenience than true security, though, because they ultimately offer another attack vector for hackers in exchange for a little less typing and memorization from their users. They are not a perfect solution, but as I discuss in later chapters of this book, no password managers are perfect security solutions.

DEADBOLTS AND 2FA

Another security measure visible to any would-be intruder is the deadbolt lock. Deadbolts are not the same as simply adding another standard lock. When a perceptive thief sees a Grade 1 deadbolt, they either search for another way in or simply move on to someone else's home or business. So not only do deadbolts upgrade security, they send a message to criminals. But deadbolts aren't the most convenient because they are a separate lock and require a different key.

Two-factor authentication (2FA) is similar to a deadbolt because it requires an additional step from its user—an additional factor. This factor can be something you know, such as a PIN, for instance; something you are, a biometric fingerprint, for instance; or something you have, a key fob, for instance. When effective 2FA is implemented, security is far more than doubled, because the chances of a hacker having your password *and* one of those factors at the ready is extremely rare. This is discussed in greater detail in a later chapter.

VIRUS-PROTECTION SOFTWARE

Malware and virus software for your PC are an important component to keep you safe. Virus software typically prevents about 20 percent of all threats; when updated regularly along with your operating system (OS) security updates, it can minimize the problems for most users. I like to think of this automated malware-scanning software as being comparable to motion-triggered camera, lighting, and alarm systems. In addition to on-site protection and deterrence, many alarm systems include twenty-four-hour security calls for an additional price. In the case of virus and malware scanners, you get twenty-four-hour service in the form of the latest updates and security patches for your computers at no extra cost.

SMARTPHONE AND TABLET RISKS

While security elements can be great deterrents in and of themselves, some homeowners can become overwhelmed by the technology or experience a false sense of security with it. I have particularly noticed this problem among users new to computers. You may wonder who that is, but I assure you that many people have avoided computers and their operating systems for most of their lives until someone gifted them a smartphone or tablet. These fairly simplistic devices are like gateway drugs that sometimes lead to harder ones.

For example, your mother-in-law might enjoy looking at photos of the grandkids on her new iPad, but she also possesses a more creative streak and wants to edit the photos as well. Many apps will do the job, but she really wants a proper photo-editing application like Adobe Photoshop. This program is not offered on mobile devices, so you buy her a modestly powered PC. From the moment she turned on that PC, she entered the world of operating systems, virus scanners, and file management. Similarly, a young student who grew up on touch-based devices is required to use a proper laptop in high school or college. They have entered the entirely new world of the power user, but we all know the quote: "With great power comes great responsibility."

BACK UP YOUR FILES

And speaking of power, what happens when burglars take their invasions to a whole new level by cutting the power to your home or building? Many internet, alarm, and telephone systems can be disabled before the thief even breaches the home perimeter. Among the truly prepared homeowner's array of fireproof safes and panic rooms resides the simple backup generator. Just a few gallons of fuel can provide hours of off-the-grid power for any home's primary defenses, as well as all the trappings of modern living.

This might seem downright extreme if not impossible, especially to someone living in an apartment building, but the digital security analogy of this protection couldn't be easier and more necessary to every computer user. Backing up your data is essentially free these days, but it's just as crucial to your online safety as ever. Large data companies give away gigabytes of free cloud storage to every customer. If you do not feel comfortable with apps that go through your photos to identify people, places, and things, then avoid using any social network offerings and services like Google Cloud. That still leaves many services available to simply back up your data with subscription tiers starting at free and going up to about ten dollars a month for terabytes of data storage.

Imagine you receive a ransomware message from a hacker asking for Bitcoin payment to release your stolen files. This is no problem if you have full backups in the cloud; you can simply ignore the message. But what if you need those files immediately for work and do not have time to download hundreds of gigabytes over a slow internet connection? Again, not a problem if you have also backed up those files to a local storage solution. External hard disk drives offer so much affordable storage that you have no excuse for not having one for both convenience and security. Besides, you should always have a backup plan that includes both on-site and off-site data backups. I'm not advocating for another generator for your home's backup generator here, but digital storage takes up no extra space, includes backup software packages from all major vendors, and has reached the point of affordability making it essentially free.

USE EMAIL FILTERS AND BEWARE OF LINKS AND ATTACHMENTS

Most email spam is akin to the junk mail we still receive in our physical mailboxes—harmless solicitations. But the cost of printing and postage has shifted to offshore email servers that are capable of much more than the simple nuisance of unwanted junk mail. Some spam email is filled with phishing attempts to lure unsuspecting computer users to click on an enticing link or attachment that leads to ransomware or worse. *Never* click on any attachment or in-message link of an email you did not expect to receive. If you wish to unsubscribe to newsletters, offers, and other spam, don't be too quick to scroll to the bottom of those emails and click on the first link you see. Many spammers have no intention of removing you from their lists, so by choosing to unsubscribe, you are validating that you are a real person who has opened and read their email.

The "email unsubscribe link," which should always be accompanied by the sender's official privacy policy and link to their address and contact information, is always a double-edged sword that can make our digital lives a little less tangled or a lot more agitated. It is up to each user to determine which spammers are genuinely innocuous or truly malicious. And if you cannot decide, a quick Google search should help shed some light onto a shady marketer.

Junk or spam email filters are extremely helpful at minimizing those unwanted solicitations that pound users and their PCs daily. These filters operate on both the server level and the local PC or device level within the email software. Server-level email filters usually apply a simple numeric scale as a threshold. How much spam can you or your business withstand? Choose "1" to allow all but the worst internet offenders into your mailbox or choose "10" to filter out every email except those from known senders. These scales come in various shapes and sizes, so be sure to consult your ISP or email server provider and be prepared to experiment a little. Everyone's tolerance for and definition of spam is a little different.

Popular browser-based email programs like Google's Gmail utilize a combination of artificial intelligence (AI) and user interaction. Gmail users begin by manually moving unwanted messages into the spam filter by right-clicking on that email. Google's AI quickly learns each user's preferences and then begins to filter unwanted messages at the server level so those types of emails never appear in your spam folder in the first place. Of course, many email programs—including Thunderbird, Outlook, and Apple Mail—also allow users to train their email clients for daily spam catching, but very few come close to the effectiveness of Google's Gmail.

Many mainstream retailers, such as Walmart, Amazon, and Target, can quickly overwhelm users with their marketing emails. These behemoths and millions of small companies that don't want to spam potential customers are subject to the same spam violation laws that every other American company must abide by. Within a business, spam reports are generally handled by a company's IT staff in order to minimize downtime and worker inefficiencies, but consumers are encouraged to report all fraudulent email messages to antifraud organizations such as spam@uce. gov and reportphishing@antiphishing.org by forwarding the entire email to them. With the exception of some lesser-known foreign companies that are not subject to the US spam and consumer protection standards, these large companies are happy to remove you from their email lists should you wish to unsubscribe at any time.

There are some clear parallels between cybersecurity and physical security that can help us all take action. We deal with the physical world and our security every day. For example, you would never leave your physical wallet unattended in public, so why would you treat your digital wallet any differently? The internet is a digital public space and cannot be treated like a safe space or like your home. Security is granted or denied based on the trust we place in the people around us. We know details about the people we invite over our homes just as they know our details. This mutually beneficial relationship is founded and built on mutual trust. Some of the people out there in the digital world are trustworthy, but that does not mean we can trust them at face value until they can prove they are who they say they are. It's much easier to get a read on someone's behavior and intent in the real world just by reading body language and facial tells and observing how they speak. The internet provides none of those options, so a little caution is always in order.

I encourage you to think like a thief and walk around your house objectively asking yourself how a thief might go about breaking in and for what purpose. Did you discover a vulnerability that you keep putting off, such as a broken lock or a poorly lit area? Take some time to shore up those vulnerabilities and if you cannot find any vulnerabilities, your local police precinct can dispatch officers who will share some of their own security observations in your home at no charge.

This same approach same holds true in our digital lives. From time to time, we need to step back to view our own digital hygiene. When was the last time you backed up your data? When was the last time you changed passwords or downloaded those nagging OS security patches? It is your duty to make both physical security and cybersecurity part of your home, business, and life so you can protect your loved ones and valuables from those that seek to take them away.

THE SHREDDER IS YOUR BEST FRIEND

Cyberthieves are criminals, and no criminals are above stealing papers found in your trash. Like spam email, we all receive physical mail littered with personal information about us, including our name, address, birth date, accounts, and credit card numbers. But unlike spam, it is relatively easy for anyone to read this personal data if we do not properly dispose of our junk mail and mail with sensitive information. If you believe that your unopened mail might be being intercepted, it could be time to plant a discreet wireless security camera to find out.

But thieves do not just intercept incoming documents delivered to your mailbox. They know the real treasure lies in outgoing papers sitting in our dumpsters and garbage cans. If you leave food scraps around the house, it will attract cockroaches or rats. And by not properly destroying sensitive documents, you can attract cyberthieves. I highly recommend getting a quality, secure paper shredder to minimize your personal data being compromised.

An array of shredders can be found at any office supply store. Most fit into one of three categories with prices ranging from $25 to $300 in all three categories, depending on the size and desired level of security: a strip-cut cuts forty to fifty strips; a cross-cut cuts two hundred small squares; and a micro-cut cuts two thousand tiny pieces of confetti.

If you do not want the hassle of buying a shredder and handling the confetti, you can also utilize a mobile shredding service that shreds and disposes of confidential documents—for a price. Much like password-management software, paper-shredding services are only as secure as their employees and protocols. If you decide on the mobile shredding route for your business or home office, research each service to verify they completely and properly shred, dispose of, and recycle all confidential documents. You might be surprised to learn that there is documentation reconstruction software that allows hackers to piece together digitally scanned strips and squares of paper. Recreating a single account number or password can justify a day of dumpster diving and shredded paper scanning for any devoted hacker. Remember, whether this data comes from an email, a text message, or a garbage can, it's all just another piece in the security puzzle about you or your business.

 POP QUIZ:

What is the simplest way to stop brute-force cyberattacks dead in their tracks?

  A. Shred all paperwork containing sensitive information.

  B. Add a deadbolt lock to all entryways.

  C. Add a few unique characters to any password or PIN.

CHAPTER 2

Spies Like OS

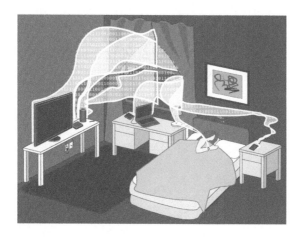

There's a hilarious scene from the classic '80s comedy *Spies Like Us* in which Chevy Chase and Dan Aykroyd brazenly cheat off each other during rigorous testing to become secret agents for the United States. Everyone sees them cheating and knows exactly what they are doing, yet they get a pass because they provide a harmless distraction while the real secret agents engage in more nefarious espionage. I cannot help but see some parallels between this funny scene and the trust we regularly have in big data and all of our digital devices. Apps, operating systems (OSs), websites, and a whole slew of software all regularly "spy" on us in order to learn more about our usage habits and provide better services, but

21

some are clearly more transparent than others when it comes to their methods and motives.

By now, many of us have seen that casual but infamous image of Facebook CEO Mark Zuckerberg sitting next to his conspicuously blinded, forward-facing laptop video camera. Even Zuck, the youngest powerful billionaire in the world, has his own privacy concerns. But are our PCs and mobile devices truly spying on us? I only wish the answer was as funny as *Spies Like Us*.

When crimes are committed, one of the first things law enforcement agents turn to for evidence is video footage. Let's face it—video cameras are becoming ubiquitous in the public arena. These surveillance systems are both obvious—with large warning signs that sometimes accompany them—and more discreet, such as cameras hidden in dark corners, in ceilings, and even inside innocent-looking devices.

ARTIFICIAL INTELLIGENCE (AI)

In September 2017, it was widely reported that China has installed more advanced public video cameras than any other place in the world. These twenty million cameras provide much more than just grainy black-and-white security footage. Each high-resolution camera is connected to a system the Chinese authorities call Skynet, an AI-based network with the ability to identify a person by their age, gender, and even particular clothing. Large networks of cameras like these are common, but tethering millions of them to a network capable of advanced machine vision is truly awe inspiring, if not worrisome, to say the least.

Large networks of cameras typically require DVRs to record and play back, which can take thousands of man-hours for subsequent law enforcement inspection. During that time, suspects and known criminals can move about, conspire with others in public, and even carry out more crimes. Without artificial intelligence, there is just too much data to comb through, giving suspects a perpetual lead on all law enforcement surveillance. And by the time agents do stumble onto valuable clues and data on the footage, it's often too late to act on the new information.

This is why AI is so valuable to tech companies, law enforcement, and even governments for surveillance purposes. What could take one thousand hours for a team of agents can literally be scanned in minutes by machines. Vast networks of cameras can automatically send alerts to law enforcement in real time through an ever-growing database of populations, license plates, and more. One of the most promising areas in law enforcement China is hoping to benefit from is fugitive tracking. These advanced systems will immediately contact local police if a suspicious individual is spotted anywhere. "Big Brother" is no longer a technological cliché reserved for the far future. However, in the case of cybersecurity, that is a good thing.

PRIVACY ISSUES

Cameras built into our personal devices also have the ability to watch us *without* our permission. Their convenience for Skyping and FaceTiming is matched only by their pervasiveness. I'm often accused of being paranoid, but I do normally keep my iMac and MacBook cameras covered. As much as I trust Apple, the possibility of security holes and malicious code getting onto my computers is very real. From there, constant surveillance of my coworkers, my family, or me is a trivial matter for an advanced hacker. Once installed on the target's PC, popular tools like Meterpreter and Kali Linux enable full remote control of a webcam, providing snapshots and livestreaming.

When Cassidy Wolf, Miss Teen USA 2013, discovered she was constantly being spied on through her computer's built-in webcam, she told CNN, "It was traumatizing." The hacker exploited a vulnerability from outdated software running on her computer. The hacker then snapped several compromising photos of her and threatened to release them and ruin her chances of winning the Miss Teen USA title. His "sextortion" crime also involved sexual favors in exchange for not releasing the photos, but Cassidy did not comply and went to the police. The hacker was caught and was sentenced to eighteen months in prison. Jared James Abrahams spied on this particular woman for over a year in addition to hacking 100 to 150 other women. This one case led to more than ninety others arrested in a global "creepware" hacker sting by the FBI.

In early 2010, Pennsylvania's Harriton High School sophomore Blake Robbins was confronted by his assistant principal. "She thought I was selling drugs, which is completely false," Blake said in an interview with CBS News. School officials admitted to capturing thousands of photos from Blake's and many other students' school-issued laptops from within their homes and elsewhere. Privacy advocates were concerned, to say the least, which eventually led to a $610,000 settlement between the school and several students.

Technology has also given employers the upper hand over their employees for years. Internet-usage monitoring, vehicle tracking, key logging, audio/video recording, and even access to medical records have all been successfully used against employees by their employers. Most companies make their employee monitoring policies clear, but even for the ones that don't, the law generally sides with employers.

EMPLOYEE MONITORING

My company has some experience with employee monitoring, or at least we sell some tools that enable other companies to survey operators over the railways. Since the introduction of smartphones, the railway industry has been increasingly fraught with accidents due to distracted operators. And like distracted car drivers, this problem is a growing epidemic. Many engineers, dispatchers, and operators of heavy machinery have succumbed to digital distractions, such as Candy Crush and Facebook, putting the lives of their crews, passengers, and the public in danger.

The Federal Rail Authority (FRA) enforces a zero-tolerance policy on distracting devices, so my company, BVS, used our wireless-security expertise to create safety products that log and alert authorities when any active cellular device is detected in a wireless-free area. This is typically accomplished by hiding our discreet receivers in the engineer's train cab and every locomotive because many operators sneak off to use their phones during long runs.

There are currently over ten thousand BVS TransitHound cell detection systems in active use on locomotives throughout the United States with another fifteen thousand orders anticipated over the next few years. "Spying" on employees to increase profits or protect the company's intellectual property, also called IP, within an organization is one thing, but monitoring employees who are failing to safely perform their duties is another issue entirely. I am proud to say that our devices have actively led to warnings and dismissals of unfit railway operators and have surely saved lives and averted untold potential in damages.

CHINA AND SPYWARE

As our smart devices continue to offload more of our private data to the cloud, more privacy abuses and infractions will surface. But as the adage goes, "If you're not paying, you're the product," so what are we really getting for our money? It's a widely held assumption that many Chinese smartphone makers, including giants like Huawei, routinely include illegal spyware on their devices. Going back to 2014, US intelligence officials from the FBI, CIA, and NSA warned that Americans shouldn't use products manufactured by certain Chinese tech companies, including ZTE and Huawei.[2] To date, US officials have not presented sufficient evidence to back such claims, but like most of us, I am willing to personally forgo some consumer convenience for the promise of increased security.

Unsatisfied with merely building every device for Chinese consumers, over the past few years, many Chinese brands have also begun aggressively targeting American consumers. In late 2017, Chinese smartphone maker Huawei overtook Apple as the world's second-largest smartphone maker with no signs of slowing down, though Samsung still holds the top spot. Brands such as OPPO, Lenovo, and Xiaomi have begun to introduce compelling features and prices to US consumers. Unfortunately, that also includes snooping apps at the Foxconn factory, which is the world's largest provider of electronics manufacturing services, headquartered in Taiwan before leaving mainland China.

2   Tom Warren, "Xiaomi Says It Plans to Enter US Smartphone Market This Year or Early 2019," The Verge, March 5, 2018, https://www.theverge.com/2018/3/5/17080146/xiaomi-us-smartphone-release-by-2019.

Security analysts have discovered spyware on most Chinese-branded smartphones, which really shouldn't come as a surprise. After all, China is notorious for spying on its own citizens in an effort to maintain order in the regime. But what possible benefit could be gained from spying on the typical American? The director of the Center for Cyber and Homeland Security, Frank J. Cilluffo, warns, "Think of it more to blackmail and recruit Americans," rather than merely spying on us. In his 2016 congressional testimony, Cilluffo pointed out that besides intellectual property (IP) theft, spying can lead to Americans acting as Chinese agents in order to avoid threats and blackmail. Hacker groups such as Deep Panda and Codoso are already believed to be used as proxies for the Chinese government. This allows China to spy on the United States with some political distancing, so it's conceivable that China would take their subcontracted spying efforts directly to the American people.

US CYBERATTACK ISSUES

Even when we dial back the cloak and dagger element for a moment, great privacy and security abuses can still originate from our personal devices. In early 2015, Lenovo laptops were discovered to contain adware that actually injected unwanted ads into users' browser sessions. Bundled software created by an advertising company called Superfish, who also created custom software called VisualDiscovery, was found to have hijacked an estimated 750,000 Lenovo customers' computers. To users, the software's effects didn't affect the browsing speed, but it was extremely invasive to the overall experience since their browsing habits were being recorded and then redirected to custom ads without their consent.

If this were the extent of the story, it really wouldn't merit much attention from cybersecurity experts, but Lenovo went much further. Not only did Lenovo try to conceal the fact from customers, but by bundling this adware, Lenovo was actually allowing this adware to act as a middleman by fooling both browsers and websites into believing user sessions were secure. The root security certificate (SSL) actually *superseded* the website's own security certificate by decrypting and re-encrypting all browser communications. So that "https" that we all look for to verify a secure connection was shown, but it was completely subverted by the advertising company Superfish, which is, thankfully, now defunct.

VisualDiscovery software essentially attacked from inside one's own hardware because it was installed at the factory level and completely invisible to users, leaving browsers vulnerable to a host of cyberattacks. When Cloudflare security researcher Marc Rogers characterized Lenovo's actions as "Quite possibly the single worst thing I have seen a manufacturer do to its customer base," he wasn't being hyperbolic.[3] Last year, Lenovo settled with the FTC for $3.5 million (paid out to thirty-six states affected) and a twenty-year risk-assessment program for software on all of its computers.

So did the punishment fit the crime in this case? After all, no one was truly harmed, as far as we know. In the digital

---

3   Maria Armental, "Lenovo Reaches $3.5 Million Settlement over Preinstalled Adware," Marketwatch.com, September 6, 2017, https://www.marketwatch.com/story/lenovo-reaches-35-million-settlement-with-ftc-over-preinstalled-adware-2017-09-05.

world, collecting and storing any personal data in a negligent manner is like leaving the gas stove on without the burner lit. It's only a matter of time before a spark comes along to ignite an explosion and, subsequently, burn everything to the ground. In this case, Lenovo wasn't just responsible for the "what if" but also responsible for deceiving their own customers. So no, the punishment didn't fit the crime, in my estimation. The FTC's punitive fine was just a slap on Lenovo's wrist and simply set a precedent for the price of doing business to any other companies watching closely.

Back in early 2012, the *New York Times* published a piece on how companies learn all of our secrets. In that article, Target was profiled for its use of advanced customer-predictive algorithms, namely a "pregnancy prediction score."[4] In this case, female shoppers were targeted with maternity products based on the likelihood that they were pregnant *and* that Target could identify the delivery date based on their shopping habits. A Target store just outside of Minneapolis received an irate phone call from a father demanding they stop mailing maternity clothing and nursery furniture advertisements addressed directly to his teenage daughter. The manager apologized profusely, even though he had nothing to do with the mailers this teenager was receiving.

Anyone possessing a Target debit or credit card is automatically profiled, tracked, and solicited. So when the store manager called back a few days later to explain the

---

4   Charles Duhigg, "How Companies Learn Your Secrets," *New York Times*, February 16, 2012, https://www.nytimes.com/2012/02/19/magazine/shopping-habits.html.

process and apologize once again, he was greeted by the same father but with a decidedly different tone. It seems that his daughter was able to keep her pregnancy a secret from the family but not from the Nicollet Mall Target store. The father apologized to the Target manager for chewing him out, and we are left with an amazing cautionary true tale of consumer privacy and the power of data gathering and artificial intelligence.

PICK YOUR POISON

So where does that leave us? Are we complicit in our spying on ourselves? We now live in a world where our digital smart speakers, like Alexa, can be used against us in court and where our faces can not only unlock our smartphones but also be tracked across the globe. We are being fed a diet of fake news, advertisements, and propaganda not only by those who would seek to harm us but also by those we pay to protect us. So many issues in life can be resolved through establishing a balance. As long as we do not put all of our privacy eggs in one basket or all of our security requirements into one resource, the worst consequences can generally be avoided. But we are now faced with many consumer choices and no clear balance among them. Choose just one digital assistant and you're still picking your poison. Amazon and Google are in millions of homes, listening all day and spitting recommended goods and services back at us.

RECENT FACEBOOK ALLEGATIONS

Facebook serves us news stories and ads based on our moods, biases, and impulses, so how can it be trusted to serve our best interests as healthy humans? I want to take a moment here to defend Facebook regarding possible spying. In light of Facebook's seemingly endless string of security and privacy blunders and breaches, they are the last company I care to defend, but let me preface by first defining it as one of the most-asked questions I continue to receive from privacy-concerned consumers. The upcoming chapter "In Big Data We Do Not Trust" goes into more detail.

For years, users have sworn up and down that Facebook is targeting ads to them based on their private verbal conversations. This pervasive rumor led New York's PIX 11 News to visit my company back in early 2018 for a TV interview.[5] Facebook has flatly denied all of the allegations in that segment and have continued to deny similar user claims made. I concluded that Facebook does have a limited ability to serve ads to individuals based on private conversations, and that Facebook does not even need to do anything so surreptitious. Facebook already has more than enough advertising data just through their growing user base of 2.3 billion monthly active users across the world. In addition, the amount of data that all of those conversations would generate could not possibly be parsed through given our current technology limitations, including device battery life being drained from continuous audio monitoring.

I suppose a small sampling of conversations could be gathered and served back to some Facebook users as ads, but let me offer a less conspiratorial viewpoint. Humans

---

5   PIX 11 News, "How Facebook Can Spy on You," February 2, 2018, https://youtu.
be/2yqx6SvqMso.

are highly susceptible to imply causation from correlation. We experience coincidences every day but generally prefer to ascribe them to something or someone with ulterior motives. It's our little way of restoring some degree of order and control to the world. Since Facebook seems hell-bent on squeezing as much profit as possible from every user, it's not a far stretch to believe they would use smartphone microphones to spy on users and then lie about it when asked. However, this assumption doesn't take the technical considerations into account nor the most logical ones either.

Through its giant social networks—consisting of Facebook, Instagram, and WhatsApp—Facebook does have full permission to track users through their online conversations, physical whereabouts, purchases originating from any of these social networks, and much more. When users speak with each other through their phones about seemingly random things, such as kitty litter, vacation getaways, and relief from back pain, and then only moments later receive ads for one of those things, they are simply playing out a narrative already in their heads. Perhaps they were already receiving some of those ads and now suddenly notice all of them since they can correlate a specific conversation back these recent ads. Perhaps a random user mentioned one of these things in a posting and the more suspicious user threw out a casual "like." With so many connections and user data under one social network, the possibilities of explanations behind these targeted ads are nearly infinite. Without proper testing and analysis, I cannot pronounce judgment with any certainty, but there's clearly a big difference between a continuously AC-powered device whose sole job is to listen for trigger words from anyone in the same room (an Amazon Echo) and a Facebook app on a smartphone that already knows everything about you without you having to say a thing.

APPLE AND USER DATA

Finally, there is Apple, the richest company in the world and also the savviest marketing company in history. But why should we believe Apple when it claims to put their customers' security and privacy first? Apple is one of the few large companies that does not profit from its users' data. Sure, it analyzes user activity on all Apple devices in order to improve products and drive more sales, but since it doesn't have a dedicated advertising platform, the company has little need to collect that data in the first place, aside from the aforementioned reason. Apple does make money from the ads its App Store developers target to users, but Apple isn't exploiting its user data in the way Google, Amazon, and Facebook all do. App Store advertising remains in a silo and is not built on the collection of data from other silos that can manipulate not just purchasing decisions but even emotions.[6]

No matter whom you trust, all of these megacorporations are vying for our attention, our loyalty, and our money. It's just that some seem to prioritize some of those things differently than others. Make no mistake:

---

6   Kashmir Hill, "Facebook Manipulated 689,003 Users' Emotions for Science," *Forbes,* June 29, 2014, https://www.forbes.com/sites/kashmirhill/2014/06/28/facebook-manipulated-689003-users-emotions-for-science/#3fbf7c52197c.

none of those companies are your friends, so ask yourself how much you trust each one and what each one asks of you. If your answer leads you to consider a life off the grid without any digital connection to people or news, you have yet another choice to make. Pick your poison carefully.

 POP QUIZ:
What's the quickest way to stop a suspected app, device, or OS from spying on you?

A. Google user reports of that device's spying activity and what those people did to stop it.

B. Log out of the suspected device or account and go about your day.

C. Visit Consumer Affairs or the Federal Trade Commission website for tips.

CHAPTER 3

Engineered for Social

All my life, I've admired my father's uncanny ability to think on his feet and get away with things most would only dream of. Gary W. Schober is an electronics engineer by trade, but that never stopped him from also being a software programmer, entrepreneur, professor, and sometimes lawyer—at least that's how he would act. He has a skillful way of wording his questions and answers to talk his way out of any precarious situation. I was always impressed by his unique ability because it seemed more like some magical gift than a skill. Some might say he cons his way around, but they would be wrong. A con artist preys on the gullibility of others by using their weakness against them. My father is honest to a fault. He merely leverages the logic of others to his favor and sometimes against them.

Late one evening back in the early 1980s, Gary was driving back from a business trip in northern New Jersey. The car he drove was remarkable at that time for its styling and engineering. A Renaissance red, manual five-speed Mazda RX-7 raced down I-287 at approximately 120 mph that night. Its Wankel rotary engine could rev forever, and I should know: this very car was my first automobile purchase from him and wouldn't be my last either.

The seemingly dark and empty road was suddenly flooded by reds and blues from behind the speeding Mazda. My father pulled over and was quickly greeted by a New Jersey state police officer.

"Sir, do you have any idea how fast you were going?"

My father quickly replied, "I have no idea, but I had to blow the carbon out of this stainless-steel exhaust."

"What do you mean?" replied the state trooper, now caught off guard.

My father went on to explain in detail the inner workings of the RX-7's unique Wankel rotary engine and how fewer moving parts—none of the valves and camshafts found in traditional cars—allowed it to spin over 10,000 rpm with additional help from an "eccentric shaft." By now, the state trooper had shifted his gestalt as authority figure to student, but before he could resume his lesson, my father threw him a second curve ball: "I was probably going so fast that only a trained state trooper could accurately assess my true speed, since radar calibration is not accurate to within plus or minus ten miles per hour unless calibrated each day."

"And how do you know this?" the perplexed state trooper asked.

"Oh, that's something my older brother told me. You see, he was a state trooper in Alaska for twenty-five years. Lonely job up there, but guess how much he pulled in last year?"

"OK, how much?"

"Seventy-five thousand a year just for arresting local drunks all day." He continued, "But he always told me the importance of opening up the engine and blowing the carbon out every so often when no one was around, so long as it was safe to speed."

"So you knew you were going over one hundred miles per hour?"

My father replied, smiling, "Of course, but I would only do this when it was completely safe late at night with no other traffic on the road but experienced drivers like you and me."

The trooper stepped back the conversation: "Alaska, huh? Tell me more about your brother."

Not only did my father not get a speeding ticket, but he ended up befriending the state trooper who pulled him over. Perhaps they bonded over my uncle's fat salary as an Alaskan state trooper, or maybe it was the radar-gun tech talk or maybe it was just the Wankel rotary engine that won over the hardened state trooper. Whatever it was, it wasn't too different than what all hackers do every day. At a fundamental level, hacking is winning your opponent's trust long enough to gain their confidence and important data in the process.

CYBER SOCIAL ENGINEERING

Back in October 2016, I had the opportunity to present at the Virginia Cybersecurity Convention in Norfolk, Virginia. The show's producers were nice enough to provide me with a stand to sell my book and also purchased fifty copies to give out to key attendees. I've done so many uncompensated appearances and contributions to shows over the years that it felt great to get some professional consideration at this event. I'm not complaining about my pro bono contributions. Those were all choices I made that led to networking opportunities and life experiences. As far as I'm concerned, I have always been compensated fairly in one way or another.

It also helps that I get to speak about subjects I am passionate about: not just the business of security, but the discipline and philosophy of cybersecurity. And even though I am often surrounded by many smart people, I rarely find myself in awe of them. That is, until I met Kevin Mitnick.

KEVIN MITNICK

Besides the distinguished title of "world's most famous hacker," Kevin is an interesting guy. In the hacker world, he needs no introduction. Still, I was happy to read through *Ghost in the Wires*,[7] his memoir detailing his various hacking scams, brush with the feds, and eventual incarceration in a federal prison. His book offers some great insights into

---

7   Kevin Mitnick, *Ghost in the Wires: My Adventures as the World's Most Wanted Hacker,* (New York: Bayback Books, 2011).

the practice of social engineering, which uses deception to manipulate individuals into divulging personal or confidential information they would not otherwise reveal.

When I was throwing around titles for my original book, phrases like *Think Like a Thief* resonated with me because I understand the deep but often misunderstood connection between hackers and thieves. Hackers are generally driven by challenges and puzzles with no particular penchant for harming others. They are tinkerers by nature but are tied to victimless crimes. Not all hackers are thieves, but most have broken the law to some degree in their hacking careers. It simply comes with the territory. Ultimately, I decided against such a title because, while I understand what it takes to accomplish such feats, I do not think like a thief except when I am trying to second-guess my defenses.

Kevin Mitnick, on the other hand, has made a career out of thinking like a thief. And while he has broken the law on several occasions, he has never financially gained directly from those actions. From an early age, Kevin Mitnick could have be an extremely wealthy man if he'd put his knowledge and skills to work for his "criminal" mind. But after his four-year stint in federal prison, which might have crushed a lesser man, he put his gray hat skills to work for white hat causes by working with the very feds who jailed him.

Kevin kicked off that Virginia Cybersecurity Convention with an energetic opening keynote speech. His social engineering lectures turn into demonstrations that then turn into full-on "hacking lessons." Mr. Mitnick's repertoire felt authentic, and his smooth approach reminds me why social engineering is the foundation for all hacking. I even volunteered to get up on stage with Kevin while he "hacked" me by using just a few basic pieces of information about me. He's a bright guy to be sure but not a math genius, as far as I can tell. His onstage demonstrations and anecdotes generally involve more verbal conversations than computer code breaking. His demeanor evokes a salesman you can trust more than a con man you might fear. Since then, I have interviewed him on several occasions and always find him engaging and sincere.

FRANK ABAGNALE JR.

If Kevin Mitnick is the world's most famous hacker, then Frank Abagnale Jr. might be the world's most infamous one. This is not to say that Frank is a bad guy, but in his youth, he lied to a lot of people and wrote even more fraudulent checks. Frank's exploits go way back to a time before hacking was even a thing, so when I met him in 2016 at the IBM i2 Summit in Washington, DC, I found a mellow older hacker with many stories and much insight into social engineering today. You can learn much more about him in *Catch Me If You Can,* the 2002 Academy Award–nominated film starring Leonardo DiCaprio and directed by Steven Spielberg. The biopic is a drama full of crimes and deceit, but to me, it was really about the power of social engineering. So when I saw Frank's keynote live, it connected some of the dots that the movie couldn't convey for a cybersecurity buff like me.

As a classic Sinatra song goes, "I've been a puppet, a pauper, a pirate, a poet, a pawn, and a king," and it could've been written about Frank Abagnale. His social engineering skills scored him gigs as a lawyer, physician, teaching assistant, and pilot, all while meticulously duplicating and forging fraudulent checks to pay his way through these faux careers. Abagnale's lies eventually landed him in prison, followed by a job working with the FBI to catch criminals doing precisely what he'd done. Frank continues to work with the bureau some forty-plus years later and still employs his same social engineering acuity and instincts to catch criminals.

The primary message in all of his presentations is that any person or organization needs to educate all of the players, from the janitorial staff to the CEO, in order to avoid being hacked. Such education prevents most security breaches, which Abagnale contends—and I also happen to agree with—are all caused by humans tricking other humans into revealing information they should not be revealing. When you strip away all of the role-playing, deceit, and stolen money, it's really that simple.

Social engineering victims come in all flavors. Some of them arm themselves against social engineers and are still fooled, while others get scammed and never even realize it. Take the hilarious segment entitled, "What is your password?" from the *Jimmy Kimmel Live!* show as evidence of the latter. This viral video featured a young woman being interviewed by one of Jimmy Kimmel's producers for his popular late-night talk show.[8]

"We are talking about cybersecurity today and about how safe peoples' passwords are," the interviewer said. "What is one of your online passwords currently?"

"It is my dog's name and the year I graduated from high school," the woman responded.

"Oh, what kind of dog do you have?" asked the interviewer.

"I have a Chihuahua–papillon," the girl sheepishly answered.

"And what's his name?"

The woman nervously smiled and said, "Jameson."

"Jameson, and where did you go to school?" asked the interviewer.

"I went to school back in Greensburg, Pennsylvania."

Without hesitation, the interviewer then asked, "What school?"

"Hipfield Area Senior High School."

"When did you graduate?" the interviewer pressed.

"In 2009," replied the woman innocently.

Of course my recounting of the dialogue doesn't do the comedy justice, nor does it tell the whole story. The

---

8   Jimmy Kimmel Live, "What Is Your Password?" January 16, 2015, https://youtu.be/opRMrEfAlil.

most effective social engineering never works as a script. Social engineering is more of an improvisational art and relies heavily on social cues. For instance, only after the interviewer lulled the woman into a more relaxed, conversational state could she then quickly follow up with more probing questions that revealed the woman's dog's name and the year she graduated. Meanwhile, the woman being interviewed didn't seem to realize she was being probed. Perhaps she was thinking of her dog or old high school friends while revealing her password to a national TV audience.

Software programmers interface with machines and code all day. They speak the language of these machines that contain priceless data, but every machine is designed for and operated by a human being. Unfortunately, these same human beings are prone to make mistakes, get distracted, and succumb to laziness or greed easily. Social engineers simply remove the middleman by bypassing the machine. They go straight to the human operator and coax them into breaking security protocols. Social engineers speak the language of people and as a result they hack people, not machines. If I had to pick just one skill to sharpen in a bag of hacking tricks, social engineering would win hands down. Whether it's hacking into a network of federal agent cell phones, posing as a Harvard graduate lawyer in the Louisiana state attorney general's office, or simply talking your way out of a speeding ticket, mastery of social engineering is always required.

POP QUIZ

What is the weakest link in cybersecurity?

A. Weak encryption.

B. Humans.

C. Short passwords.

CHAPTER 4

Minding the Hack

The idioms "Put yourself in my shoes" or "Walk a mile in someone else's moccasins" are typically meant to elicit a higher degree of empathy, but these expressions can also be used to help you protect your small business and personal data. Sometimes the best way to avoid, beat, or capture a hacker is to think like one. When we better understand the motives and reasons behind cybercriminals' actions, we can build strong defenses to deter them so they will move on to easier targets. Indirectly sending criminals in someone else's direction is an unfortunate side effect, but to my knowledge, it remains the most effective way to stay safe yourself. As soon as I figure out a way to warn the rest of the world—besides this book—I will get right on it.

The first step in getting into the hacker mind-set is exercising a proper level of detachment. For instance, I am able to marvel at the ingenuity and persistence of a skilled hacker without agreeing with their politics or condoning their criminal activities. It's as important as having a discussion with someone you might normally disagree with. You don't have to agree that their favorite sports team is the best or that their choice of smartphone is superior. You don't even have to like them, but by listening to their reasoning, you can prepare and apply those same approaches to your own counterarguments. Just like the Japanese martial art of Aikido, using your opponent's energy and tactics against them can be a most effective form of offensive defense. And since we are all consumers and internet users, cybercriminals are able to predict our next few moves much like a chess master.

HACKING APPROACHES

Hackers make decisions based on trust and the information internet users willingly put out there. Good hackers use our innate human weaknesses in order to exploit them. By creating a false sense of urgency, they can manipulate victims into reacting or possibly overreacting. If we remove the hacker from the scenario, simply reacting (or even overreacting) to one's security shortcomings is a positive move. Now place the hacker back into the scene, and a completely different series of events unfolds.

RANSOMWARE

Unfortunately, cyberattacks are now a foregone conclusion. With ransomware, the cybercriminals have already stolen the data, but it has no value to them other than the victim's response. After the data has been compromised and encrypted, the hacker's only goal is to drive up the cost of the ransom by engineering emotional arcs.

This approach is similar to some of our favorite serialized streaming TV shows. The most popular ones have conditioned their loyal viewers to believe that the main characters cannot possibly confront their demons and mend their relationships until the climax of an episode or an entire season. The more skillful the storyteller, the less obvious the artificial-narrative constructs appear, but make no mistake, the constructs are always there. Consider any action movie involving a bomb on a timer. Our hero already has their hands full with bad guys at large, a loose cannon of a partner, and innocent civilians in the mix. This is normally enough to make most of us want to run away crying from the situation, but throw in a bomb set to go off at noon and you suddenly have an intensified situation for the sole purpose of emotionally charging the story. Ransomware hackers employ these very same techniques. The arbitrary use of a countdown clock common in most ransomware only serves to up the tension while simultaneously tricking the victims into action (in the form of Bitcoin payout) based on their fear rather than logic. Logic would dictate that ransomware victims should always contact law enforcement, retrace their digital steps, and lock down the data they still control.

More details on ransomware are found in the upcoming chapter, "Opening a Can of Cyber Worms."

PHISHING

Phishing is a scam by which an internet user is duped or lured into clicking an email link or attachment (generally through a deceptive email message) with the ultimate goal of having the victim reveal personal or confidential information the scammer can use illicitly. One would think that the sheer number of interactions we have on a daily basis would only slow our appetite for the proper content, when in fact the opposite holds true. The internet is a buffet of choices, and when we see a fantastic bargain in a believable email, we tend to click on it, and before you know it, we have logged into a phony website and handed over personal and financial data. This all transpires in a matter of minutes but could have been bypassed in even less time. It takes only seconds to peruse an email for telltale signs of phishing and even less time to type the URL directly into our browsers.

I recently witnessed this lack of patience firsthand when my eleven-year-old son played into the hands of a cyberthief. One of his favorite games on the Xbox is *Rocket League*, a fast-paced action game that substitutes professional athletes for souped-up sports cars in a multiplayer online virtual soccer match. The game also allows for customizable cars with features earned only through hours and hours of game play and trading digital assets to other players. In my son's eagerness to trade some of his own customizations for another player's, he sent over fifteen items to that player in good faith. He never received any of the promised digital merchandise back, instead receiving only a simple message reading "LOL" followed by that player's logging off the Xbox Live network.

He was heartbroken but rather than letting this breach of trust dishearten him, I decided to use it as a teaching moment. We both stepped through everything that happened to look for the signs. We followed that up by sending an abuse report on that gamer and all the details to Xbox Live. Beyond that, there was little we could do, but it's important that my son realize that the anonymity of Xbox Live and the internet as a whole sometimes fosters bullies, criminals, and frauds of all kinds. My only consolation is that he learned this lesson early with minimal loss.

Hackers can effectively and quickly exploit their victims' fight-or-flight instincts instead of letting them take more time to question their next step, but other hackers also work the long game. Social engineering is a ubiquitous skill among hackers, but very few have the patience to slowly harvest victims. Many internet users make quick decisions based on familiarity, but most people still deal with trusted sources, have face-to-face contact with others, and rely on a network of friends and family to help them through challenges.

Other users are less fortunate. Many on social networks have shut themselves off from regular interpersonal interactions. Since the early 2000s, psychologists have warned that the "disinhibition effect" associated with the internet comes with both pros and cons. Similar to the effects of alcohol consumption, the anonymity of online interactions can lower social barriers and reveal secret fears and dreams. But this same catharsis can also allow users to become targets for those looking to exploit those same fears and dreams.

CATFISHING

Catfishing lures someone into an online relationship by way of a fictional persona, and it tends to happen over time. Catfishing is simply a new-tech twist on an old con involving trust, anonymity, and at least one gullible victim. Online catfishing became popular just as social networks like Facebook, Twitter, and Instagram came into their own. There is even a long-running show called *Catfish* on MTV. The victims tend to place more importance than they should on virtual relationships, and they project their own desires onto this nonexistent "person." But unlike most other cons, catfishing has no real monetary agenda. Sometimes money or gifts are promised and exchanged, but the majority of these encounters only exploit emotions and make dead-end promises.

No one deserves to be catfished, even if there is no theft, which makes catfishers' motives all the more questionable and insidious. What kind of person takes pleasure in stringing others along only to break their hearts? I would contend that both parties are damaged in different ways. One is a perpetual victim, and the other is simply another kind of bully.

CYBERBULLIES

The playground bullies from yesteryear have evolved into the cyberbullies of today. These people might not be hackers in the technical sense, and they certainly aren't hackers in the playful and exploratory nature of many hackers, but cyberbullies employ similar techniques to those of misguided, black hat hackers. They take what does not belong to them and receive further satisfaction from knowing they got into someone's head.

Many illegal hackers also prefer to sneak into and trespass through the victim's computer undetected. While that might not appear to be the overly aggressive acts of a bully, do not be fooled. Like vandals wielding spray paint, they generally leave their calling cards somewhere. Sometimes buried in a line of malware code and sometimes in a pseudonymous ransomware letter, many hackers cannot resist the urge to mark their turf. This functions as a warning to their victims and also gives them bragging rights to "impress" the rest of the hacker community.

STATE-SPONSORED HACKS

Notes and manifestos are also typically found at the virtual scene of the crime in cases of larger security breaches. Remember the Sony breach by the Guardians of Peace hacker group just before Sony Pictures' release of *The Interview?* The comedy saw limited theatrical distribution due to terrorist threats of violence in movie theaters across the country because it depicted the assassination of North Korean leader Kim Jong-un. After several communications from the hackers and an analysis by FBI behavioral analysts, US authorities concluded that the hacks and subsequent threats originated from North Korea. Even if their motives and demands were dubious, North Korea fired back by denying any involvement in the hacks and deemed the hack a "righteous deed." The United States levied sanctions against North Korea, and the story ended there because the responsible parties were never identified or brought to justice.

Many hackers feel the need to justify their actions by moralizing against their targets. If it's a government target, usually an opposing state sponsored it—complete with political rhetoric, as was the case with the 2015 hack of the US Central Command's Twitter account by ISIS's own Cyber Caliphate.

HACKING MOTIVATIONS

And some hacker groups target their own governments in an effort to call attention to a perceived wrong. In December 2017, "Anonymous" hacked a US government database and released the addresses of dozens of FCC staff, including Chairman Ajit Pai. Since the names are public knowledge and mostly searchable through Google, the privacy violation was minimal, but nevertheless, Anonymous was punished by Twitter for violating its policies. The last Anonymous tweet before an eleven-hour silence read, "We already knew this would happen before we tweeted it out that's why we like to say that we took this sacrifice with a lot of pride. Keep fighting for the Internet our home! #OpDefendTheNet #NetNeutrality #Anonymous"

HACTIVISM

Like a cyber Robin Hood, groups like Anonymous thrive on the public attention and overtures of social justice when they practice their own brand of hacktivism. Coined in 1992, hacktivism means disruptively hacking for a "moral reason" and to effect social change. These hackers present their point of view as speaking truth to power, and they challenge authorities on moral grounds. In the case of Anonymous, their public outcry against the dissolution of net neutrality by the FTC in June 2018 actually aligned with the American public and not their own government. Net neutrality meant that internet service providers (ISPs) were required to treat all data traveling over their networks the same. Without the net neutrality rules, they no longer have to treat all internet traffic equally and will be able to prioritize certain websites and services over others.

Such groups are decentralized to prevent corruption from the top, ensure their anonymity, and avoid division within the ranks. This approach is a dual-edged sword. On the one hand, it can create chaos within and around the group's efforts, making it difficult to stage an effective campaign against their enemy. On the other hand, like conventional terrorism, hactivism creates a media sensation and stirs many disenfranchised people into action.

This is clear when you examine the ages and genders of the quintessential hacker. Young males are typically recruited by these groups for their aggression, their aimlessness, and ultimately, their desire to fit into a group in some capacity. When they were young, now-famous hacker icons such as Kevin Mitnick, Albert Gonzalez,

Julian Assange, Kevin Poulsen, and Robert Tappen Morris all began their hacking exploits in their teens and early twenties. So when news feeds of them being hauled off by the authorities in handcuffs went public, it served only as a recruitment tool for thousands of other disenfranchised, computer-literate youths looking to make their own impact.

CYBERCRIME AND THE FUTURE

Headlines like "Cybercrime damages are predicted to cost the world $6 trillion by 2021"[9] may seem hyperbolic but make sense on further inspection. In Cybersecurity Ventures' *2017 Official Annual Cybercrime Report*, the $6 trillion figure is up from $3 trillion in 2015.[10] Compared to conventional crime, cybercrime is a new business model for crooks, so doubling revenue over six years seems to fit its growth expectation. I'm not trying to minimize this staggering figure but rather put it into perspective. The world of business and commerce is full of bottom-feeders of all shapes and sizes. It's only natural that as business grows, so do they. But it's also natural that the old world of business with paper contracts, steel vaults, and armed security forces naturally evolves with the world of phishing scams, cryptocurrency, and cybercrime AI. Global

---

9   Cybersecurity Ventures, "Cybercrime Damages Are Predicted to Cost the World $6 Trillion by 2021," PR Newswire, October 17, 2017, https://www.prnewswire.com/news-releases/cybercrime-damages-are-predicted-to-cost-the-world-6-trillion-annually-by-2021-300540158.html.

10   Cybersecurity Ventures and Herjavec Group, 2017 Official Annual Cybercrime Report, October 2017, https://cybersecurityventures.com/2015-wp/wp-content/uploads/2017/10/2017-Cybercrime-Report.pdf.

business is growing and shifting to digital transactions and currencies, and the crime follows.

BUG BOUNTIES

"Bug bounties" are prizes awarded to individuals or security groups who demonstrate a major security flaw in a company's network or product, and they work. The term "bug bounty" was first coined by Netscape engineer Jarrett Ridlinghafer back in 1995 when the company officially launched its program. Since then, major tech companies, including Google, Apple, Microsoft, and Facebook, have been lining up to create their own private and public bug bounty initiatives with payouts typically ranging from $10,000 up to $250,000, depending on the nature of the exploit. Many of the participating hackers use the awards to supplement their regular salaries, but bug bounties aren't always just about the money. What motivates these hackers to fight back by alerting companies to security holes?

In the *2016 Bug Bounty Hacker Report*, the 617 hackers surveyed revealed that 72 percent hack for money, 70 percent for fun, and 65 percent to build a résumé.[11] Though many of these hackers typically come from a black hat background, all of them now identify as white hats or at least gray hats, which illustrates a level of maturity not often found in hacker communities. In fact, the surveyed bug bounty hackers ranged across more than seventy countries with a median age of twenty-six—which is young but slightly

---

11   HackerOne, 2016 Bug Bounty Hacker Report, September 13, 2016, https://www. hackerone.com/blog/hacker-surey-report-2016.

older than most black hats—and it shows. When asked why they hack, over 50 percent responded, "To do good in the world." Fifty-seven percent of bug bounty hackers did not even participate in programs that pay out rewards. The cynical and dangerous inclinations of the "hack back" political movement are being schooled by the entrepreneurial and proactive approach of bug bounty programs.

MY EXPERIENCE

In April 2018, my small business was the victim of a targeted spoofing attack. For such an attack to be successful, the hacker needed insights on my industry's business, products, and sales channels. Only then could a hacker tailor an effective email spoof that could fool my business partners and break down the digital barriers, allowing them to ultimately steal money. In the end, they did not steal any money from my business or sales partners, but it doesn't mean I won that round either. Since the hacker began by expertly spoofing my company's email, he gained a degree of trust from many of my international resellers. In fact, out of my seventy-plus international resellers, eight of them contacted me about receiving a suspicious email, and four had even corresponded with the hacker before alerting me. The emails involved a $78,000 transaction fee, which is typical for any of my resellers. However, a few astute sales partners recognized typos, grammatical errors, and even that the email contained an extra letter in my name—a sure tip-off. Unfortunately, the domain was correct, which let the email pass through most of their junk-mail filters.

I receive hundreds of spam and fraudulent emails every day, so why did this one feel more like a violation than all the others? Because this hacker managed to penetrate my inner circle of trusted colleagues and business partners. And if any of them could be fooled, even briefly, it means maybe my loved ones and I could be fooled too.

In July 2018, Twitter reportedly suspended over seventy million fake accounts. Out of Twitter's total 330 million user accounts, the fake ones are 20 percent of the total user base. Just imagine how you would feel if you discovered that one out of every five of your friends wasn't even a real person and had been lying to you from day one. Of course, most of us treat our physical friends differently than our online ones, but as the two worlds continue to merge, we can expect incidents of fraud, theft, and even heartbreak to rise sharply. But are we all doomed to be taken by faceless hackers and their spam bots and malware?

Hacking will always be a simple extension of humanity. Like any tool, it will lead to both positive and negative consequences. The motives behind the hackers and their tools are worth examining because they hold up a mirror to our society, our businesses, and ourselves. And when we look into that mirror, we see all of our common instincts, the good intentions alongside the greed and nihilism. We also see our own flaws staring back at us. Sometimes it takes only a warning or a threat to secure our business. Other times a security expert or penetration tester will help reveal the weaknesses we refuse to see for ourselves. Sometimes it even takes an all-out attack before we shore up our cyber defenses. Those same flaws, apparent to anyone else looking for our weaknesses, can be improved on, cast aside, and even fully replaced but only if we are willing to briefly step into the mind of a hacker.

 POP QUIZ:

What is the first thing you should do if your company is facing ransomware demands?

A. Determine whether the ransomware demand is legitimate and follow the instructions to get your data back.

B. Ignore the demands but back up all data just in case.

C. Contact police and do not pay the ransom.

CHAPTER 5

You're in Good Hands with Cyber Insurance

We are all familiar with health insurance, mortgage insurance, life insurance, and home insurance. Now we need to add cybersecurity to the growing list of insurances. On the surface, cyber insurance may appear like another insurance company money grab, but dig a little deeper and you will realize it's also a necessity in today's digital world. Car insurance is required for every driver on the road, so it's not such a stretch to foresee a time when every internet user—or at least every small business owner—will be required to obtain cyber insurance.

Nowhere is insurance against hackers and breaches more important than to small businesses. According to the *Ponemon Institute 2016 Cost of Data Breach Study*, nearly 63 percent of all small businesses became targets of breaches or have incurred a loss of data.[12] And more than half of those small businesses attacked also close down within a few months. Larger corporations can withstand some heavy losses and have staying capacity, whereas smaller businesses do not have the reserves and are the first ones to go under.

While cyber insurance is becoming more widely accepted, it is not yet prevalent. The biggest problem most US firms have with cyber insurance is that they don't see the value. Half of all US companies do not have cyber insurance, and 27 percent of executives say they have no plans to take out such insurance, yet 61 percent of them also expect cyber breaches to increase this year. There is a strong disconnect between reality and business planning here. According to a survey conducted recently by research firm Ovum, about 40 percent of UK and Canadian firms have no cyber insurance coverage, so they are in only a slightly better position than US corporations should they suffer a cyberattack.[13]

---

12   LLarry Ponemon, Ponemon Institute, Ponemon Institute 2016 Cost of Data Breach Study, June 16, 2016, https://www.ponemon.org/news-2/23.

13   *Insurance Journal*, "Why 27% of U.S. Firms Have No Plans to Buy Cyber Insurance," May 31, 2017, https://www.insurancejournal.com/news/national/2017/05/31/452647.htm.

Over the years, I've spoken to many individuals who know the risks and percentages but still do not act (or possibly feel) as if they are in danger of attacks and breaches. They seem to think they're already doing enough to protect themselves and that cybercriminals will leave them alone for other more likely targets. These are individuals with no employees, customers, or business overhead, so their ignorance is almost understandable. But how do you convince an executive in charge of departments, payrolls, pensions, and confidential data to take action when they *know* they're on deck to be the next big data breach? More than half of these small businesses will be compromised. That's worse than the odds of a coin flip! And yet complacency, poor budgeting, and lack of foresight will keep most of these businesses in hackers' lines of sight. It seems that at the very least, a responsible business should explore the possibility of cyber risk insurance.

On the other end of the spectrum are the business owners who don't hesitate to pay for a cyber insurance policy or research implementing the necessary security changes before and during that policy's duration. Most auto insurance policies cover damage or harm inflicted by drivers operating unsafe vehicles or even in an intoxicated state, but cyber insurance does not work that way. Qualified security assessors require proof that credit card transactions are handled only by approved employees in predesignated areas of a business, for example. Requirements like this have been enforced since 2004, according to standard Payment Card Industry Data Security Standard (PCI DSS) compliance policies, so they have been carried over to many cyber insurance policies too.

If employers do not comply with fire safety standards and they open a claim with their fire insurer, they will not be covered or compensated in the event of a fire. The same thing can be said of cyber insurance, which usually affects much more than just the employer's business. Any business owners regularly handling private data owe it to their customers to treat said data with approved security standards, not simply to collect insurance damages but to stop their customers' private data from being spread all over the internet and ruining lives further.

CYBER INSURANCE REQUIREMENTS

Contrary to most small business owners' beliefs, they do have many things worth stealing. The idiom "One man's trash is another man's treasure" not only applies here but is how most hackers get their start. Going through anyone's physical trash can reveal a great deal about them personally, but going through a small business owner's trash can also reveal a great deal about anyone they do business with. Financial statements, emails, phone numbers, Social Security numbers, and banking account numbers are just a few items that can be gathered from a brief dumpster dive. Since no office is completely paperless, the need for a decent paper shredder is both advisable and required by some cyber insurance brokers.

Hard drives, current PCs, old computers, and external enclosures must be secured for any cyber insurance broker to even consider covering a small business. It's no different than refusing fire insurance to a claimant that does not comply with basic fire safety regulations. Data is the lifeblood of all businesses, whether it's customer data, financial data, or intellectual property. All data has value to someone, therefore all businesses are potential targets. If a business owner still doesn't make the connection between his or her liabilities and responsibilities, I ask some of the following questions:

- Do you have insurance for your home, business, or car?

- Do you have personal information on your employees stored anywhere?

- Do you store client and vendor information, such as credit cards?

- Are you PCI compliant? (the payment card industry data security standard)

- How do you store and destroy documents?

- What is your data backup plan? Are all of your backups on-site?

- Have you participated in any cybersecurity training to discuss best practices?

- Do you have a "bring your own device" (BYOD) policy?

Specific technical questions like these can sometimes trigger a less defensive response. It might also help that I'm not an insurance salesperson but rather a fellow business owner or colleague. If they still won't relent, I get more personal.

POTENTIAL COST OF NO CYBER INSURANCE

If you are anything like me, the mere mention of insurance and premiums sends a chill down your spine. Up until Superstorm Sandy hit my home state of New Jersey in 2012, insurance was just a necessary evil that responsible adults had to put up with, but that natural disaster reminded me that real people trying to do their best jobs played a big role in the recovery. The storm took 233 lives and wreaked over $75 billion in damages to New Jersey and New York. My home and our entire nearby building went without power for eleven days. After the basic safety of my family and our corporate headquarters was taken into account, my next challenge was making sure our thirty employees would continue to get paid during the shutdown.

Once I was able to secure payroll, I contacted my insurance company to see what kind of provisions were available for our small business. Their agents wasted no time in coming out, interviewing me for our needs, and assisting us with those eleven days of lost revenue during the forced shutdown. I suspect many small businesses teetering on the edge of collapse were fiscal victims of the 2012 storm. Fortunately, we were healthy enough to withstand the impact and, thanks to the quick response of our insurance company, we were able to bounce back swiftly.

Many small businesses today are also teetering on the edge of collapse due to cybersecurity vulnerabilities and the lack of insurance for the inevitable breaches resulting from those same vulnerabilities. The list of respected cybersecurity experts proclaiming "not if, but when" breaches will occur is far too long. And experts like

Cisco's John Chambers go further: "There are two types of companies: those that have been hacked and those who don't know they have been hacked."

Imagine if catastrophic weather systems were as easy to predict. Now imagine that nearly all meteorologists could predict major flooding in your town. Would you continue to procrastinate on obtaining flood insurance? No. We have essentially arrived at this point in cybersecurity. After answering my list of insurance questions, the only question left in a small business owner's mind should be, *Where do I sign up?*

BREACH NOTIFICATION LAWS

Many business insurance carriers already require a minimum of $50,000 in cyber risk coverage *before* they will provide the more conventional insurance. When your business suffers a data leak, you are quickly reminded that anything unrelated to your primary business is just a distraction, and distractions can kill otherwise healthy businesses. These distractions may include cyber insurance, but you still need to adhere to the breach notification laws for notifying states of cyberbreaches. Since the majority of small business owners are unfamiliar with their state's requirements, CEOs can quickly find themselves caught up in red tape and regulations. So it is important to clearly acknowledge and understand those laws *before* a breach occurs.

According to the breach notification laws in forty-eight states, a business owner must inform all concerned entities that the business's personal information (PI) has been compromised. PI includes, but is certainly not limited to, bank account numbers, credit card numbers, associated PINs, expiration dates, Social Security numbers, and driver's license numbers. Breach notification laws require businesses to contact each and every entity and inform them *what* was compromised, *when* it occurred, and the *prevention techniques* to keep this from reoccurring.

Each company needs to carefully find the best insurance plan relevant to the specific risk that company may be exposed to. Therefore, business owners should factor in their specific industries and the size of their businesses. A trusted insurance broker can help you gain a better understanding of what works best for your business; allowing them into your business-growth model will help them tailor a cyber policy to meet your current and future needs. When you have an expert to break down what is covered—and just as importantly, what is *not* covered— you can make a sound business decision to adequately protect your business while minimizing your risk.

Not all cyber breaches are motivated from the same place either. In 2017, food giant Mondelez reported $100 million in damages inflicted on its network by a particularly insidious ransomware attack known as NotPetya. This ransomware disrupted Mondelez's factory production on a massive scale by spreading malware across vulnerable Windows PCs, overwriting the existing bootloader (a program that loads the operating system when the computer is turned on) with a custom one, and demanding $300 in Bitcoin. Unfortunately for Mondelez, the US government has classified this attack as a coordinated military effort by the Russian government.

Russia denies the claims, but Mondelez's cyber insurance company, Zurich Insurance Group, considered NonPetya cyberattacks to be an act of war, which voids the insurance claim.[14] While this is an isolated incident and will probably not have any lasting ramifications on small businesses, it does force cyber insurance providers to consider their positions more carefully, if not at least clarify their coverage clauses.

HOME OFFICE CYBER RISKS

With many employees working from home offices, it is essential to shore up your home cyber defenses as well. American International Group (AIG) offers personal cybersecurity insurance called Family CyberEdge. If your home falls victim to a cyberattack, AIG offers legal services and a home assessment for all electronic devices, including computers and Wi-Fi routers. While this insurance is not for everyone, it's essential if you work from home and/or have remote access to your company's computer network. Your home computer, Wi-Fi router, and any mobile devices can all be conduits for breaches, ultimately leaving you or your company to clean up the mess. Therefore, having a professional third party help you create strong passwords, perform basic penetration testing, and conduct regular security audits can go a long way.

---

14   Charlie Osborne, "NotPetya an 'Act of War,' Cyber Insurance Firm Taken to Task for Refusing to Pay Out," ZDNet, January 11, 2019, https://www.zdnet.com/article/notpetya-an-act-of-war-cyber-insurance-firm-taken-to-task-for-refusing-to-pay-out/.

BEST CYBERSECURITY PRACTICES

In order to comply with most cybersecurity insurance coverage requirements, you must complete a checklist verifying the implementation of best cyber practices within your organization. Honesty and transparency are imperative at this stage because any misrepresentation can result in denial of future claims.

For example, you will likely need to relay how you typically handle data destruction of paper documents containing employee personal information or client credit cards. There will be questions concerning your bring your own device (BYOD) policy and its subsequent restrictions. For example:

- Do you perform simulated phishing attacks to test employee response and share the results with all employees?

- Do you educate all employees on password creation and management?

- Have you drafted a plan for employees to easily and immediately report possible cyber threats or dangers?

Cybersecurity might be everyone's business, but that doesn't mean obtaining cyber insurance is always a slam dunk. Since I am not an insurance expert, I can only refer you to one to investigate the possibility of cyber insurance. As a business owner for decades, I've seen fads come and go, so I'm sure you will agree with me that things like computer networks and threats to sensitive and proprietary data are here to stay.

POP QUIZ:

Which one of these things will a comprehensive cyber insurance policy NOT protect you from?

A. Poor cybersecurity hygiene and implementation.

B. A ransomware attack on your company's computer network.

C. An employee skimming/stealing customers' credit cards.

CHAPTER 6

Do Not Read This Chapter until You've Done Just One Small Thing

Right now, I want you to put this book down and do one simple thing for me: log in to one of your accounts on your smartphone or computer, navigate to the security settings, and just change the password. Go ahead, I'm waiting . . .

If you simply change one password today, you will improve your personal and/or small business's security and substantially decrease the chances of being hacked. How do I know this? Because I've been hacked—due to weak password protection—and also because you have already been hacked and just do not know it. Just because your bank account hasn't been depleted or your social media profile hasn't been hijacked does not mean you have not already been hacked.

Still don't believe me? Try visiting the website www. HaveIBeenPwned.com, and like most new visitors to that website, you will discover that your email address has been associated with several breached websites. If your email has no connection to any breached sites, congratulations, but that only means you are next in line to be hacked because billions upon billions of passwords, emails, and other critical security identifiers are being put up for sale across the Dark Web at this moment. Hacking begins long before the victim is ever aware of a hack. Otherwise, hackers would only be a trivial nuisance like houseflies buzzing around. Want to know how to make hackers as trivial as houseflies?

By now, you've either written me off as a paranoid crackpot (you wouldn't be the first) or you're getting that nervous sweat forming down the back of your neck. I've experienced the latter more than I care to remember, so I know the feeling of personal invasion you might be experiencing. Let me assure you that I am not attempting to needlessly scare my readers into action. I want you to know that you do have control of your digital life; all you need to do is follow through on the tools already in place and waiting for you to take action.

THE PROBLEM WITH PASSWORDS

While the first verbal passwords probably date back to prehistory, passwords that unlock the conveniences of modern life have been around for nearly sixty years. Ninety-one-year-old American scientist Fernando Corbato has been credited as the creator of the modern password. "The password has become kind of a nightmare," Corbato admits in an interview with the *Wall Street Journal* a few years ago. He went on to reveal that he had personally been using a crude handwritten sheet containing 150 of his own passwords.[15] According to a 2017 report from LastPass, the average business user manages 191 passwords, so Fernando Corbato is not alone in his nightmare.[16]

Between my business and personal life, I use about two hundred passwords regularly, but I can still recall the hassle of remembering my four-digit debit card PIN back in the 1980s for ATMs. Passwords have come a long way since then, but users have not evolved nearly as fast. According to most psychological experiments, the human brain has difficulty memorizing and recalling more than seven digits. That's fine for rattling off telephone numbers, but eight characters is considered the absolute minimum security

---

15   Danny Yadron, "Man Behind the First Computer Password: It's Become a Nightmare," *Wall Street Journal*, May 21, 2014, https://blogs.wsj.com/digits/2014/05/21/the-man-behind-the-first-computer-password-its-become-a-nightmare/.

16   Amber Gott, "LastPass Reveals 8 Truths about Passwords in the New Password Exposé," LastPass, November 1, 2017, https://blog.lastpass.com/2017/11/lastpass-reveals-8-truths-about-passwords-in-the-new-password-expose.html/.

standard for any password these days. I personally aim for twelve random character passwords that can include all thirty-six uppercase and lowercase alphanumeric characters, as well as special characters. This ensures that brute-force attacks by the most advanced graphic processing units (GPUs) will take years, not weeks, to crack my passwords.

Any website, app, or social media service worth visiting requires at least twelve-character passwords, but many of these companies fear that users valuing convenience—meaning the ability to memorize and quickly recall passwords—over their own security will move to competing services with easier logins. This creates a race to the bottom, where the winner attracts the most users, the most hackers, and, as a result, the most hacking victims.

PASSWORD SPRAYING

In early 2018, the United States Computer Emergency Readiness Team (US-CERT) issued a threat alert about "password spraying," an attack attempting to access a large number of accounts/usernames with a few common passwords. Since most modern systems limit the number of login attempts by forcing users to wait a set amount of time before they try to log in again, password spraying attempts to circumvent this limitation by exploiting laziness.

Password spraying uses only a single weak, commonly used password against multiple user accounts. This method is effective because it instantly identifies user accounts still using default admin passwords or perhaps one of the top ten most common weak passwords, such as PASSWORD123. The only thing a hacker employing password spraying really needs is a lot of emails and a cloud-based service to target. Since they are attempting only one login per user, the network does not view this as suspicious. Fortunately, passwords aren't the only factor required for most logins these days.

THE LATEST AUTHENTICATIONS

Aside from complex passwords, this increasingly popular security requirement might seem like an undue burden at first, but it's really the closest thing we currently have to bulletproof password protection if we understand its limitations. Two-factor authentication (2FA) is a method of confirming user identity by using a combination of two different factors, such as something only you know, like a password; something you have, such as your smartphone; and something unique to you, like your fingerprint. All big data tech companies now require 2FA in order to log in to any of their services.

When *Hacked Again* was released back in March 2016, Apple had still not required two-step authentication for logging into their services, which demonstrates how quickly the industry must adopt and push new standards to keep their billions of users secure. In fact, chapter 22 of *Hacked Again* was all about Apple's iCloud hack that revealed nude celebrity photos. The fact that Apple arrived a little late to the 2FA party is no coincidence, because the same hackers that socially engineered celebrity passwords also relied on the fact that those same celebrities had not set up their iCloud accounts to require an additional identity factor.

So while iCloud was never actually hacked, the *individual* account hacks would have likely been prevented had Apple required 2FA sooner.

Not all companies define this additional layer of protections exactly the same. The important takeaway is that two-step authentication (2SA) and two-step verification (2SV) have been replaced by the more secure 2FA that requires a hardware device or biometric input, such as a facial or iris scan, in addition to a password to fully verify the user.

AUTHENTICATION CODES

Every advance in security technology also brings new exploits and possible chinks in the armor. While 2FA is robust, many services now allow users to receive tokenized authentication codes on their devices via SMS text messages. Unfortunately, hackers have repeatedly demonstrated the ability to intercept incoming text messages, as well as clone user devices to receive the codes before users even realize something is amiss. This is not a weakness in the smartphone hardware per se, but if your authentication device relies on your wireless carrier's SMS to deliver 2FA codes, your second authentication factor can be compromised.

This is just one more reason why I feel safer living in an Apple ecosystem. Apple's Messages app sends end-to-end encrypted texts among Apple devices via Apple's secure network. Unlike any wireless carriers' SMS texts that can be spoofed and possibly intercepted, Apple's Messages has not succumbed to this fate. If you receive a green bubble text on your iPhone, that means it originated from a non-

Apple device or it originated from an Apple device that was not logged into Messages. Blue bubbles are totally secure. Beware of the green bubbles—just kidding, but not really.

SECURITY TOKENS/FOBS

Aside from devices themselves, many enterprise logins and authentications are accomplished through security tokens or key fobs. These physical devices are similar to USB sticks in size but generate tokenized codes for each and every login to ensure the right person is accessing the right account. Some are used in place of passwords, but the truly secure methods use them in addition to a password. Cryptographic passwords are generated either randomly or through a timer whose clock is synchronized to the server that the user is trying to connect to.

WEBAUTHN

As of this writing, the World Wide Web Consortium (W3C) approved a new authentication standard called WebAuthn. This security standard aims to replace our reliance on passwords to access online accounts by utilizing an application programming interface (API) that supports physical security keys and biometric inputs. It's still in early days, but the standard has been approved by all major browsers and is already being used by Dropbox and Microsoft. If WebAuthn catches on, we could see an end to memorized passwords. However, we could also find ourselves fumbling around for that damn security key every time we want to check our email, so I will reserve my judgment until I see a convenient yet secure implementation across a major platform.

BEHAVIORAL BIOMETRICS

Behavioral biometrics is an exciting area that provides additional security over traditional passwords without the complexity of additional codes or devices. The one thing you always have is your fingerprint, iris, and face. There are 240 distinct features unique to every person in an iris scan, which is five times more distinguishing than fingerprint scans. And while no security system is 100 percent secure, the rate of false positives for iris scanning is estimated to be one in one million, which offers me some solace.

The aspect of biometrics that does not give me a warm and fuzzy feeling is the same one that makes it so convenient. As annoying as they are, I can always change my passwords if they are hacked or required to be reset or updated for newer security standards. But I cannot change my iris, fingerprint, or face without complex, expensive, and potentially dangerous cosmetic surgical procedures. I was never more aware of this fact than when I copresented at the 2018 RSA Conference—the world's leading information security conference that brings some forty-five thousand top cybersecurity professionals and business leaders together—with Tyler Cohen Wood on the security implications of biometric implants. Tyler is a former senior intelligence officer for the Defense Intelligence Agency, so she's been through plenty of security portals and searches in her day. My knees tend to buckle at the sight of blood, and I get especially queasy with the idea of anything implanted just under the skin. Nevertheless, I can envision a near future in which biometric implants will become as widely accepted and prevalent as tattoos have become over the past decade.

I was reluctant to include a chapter in this book about passwords since they are boring, overplayed, and generally ignored by most readers, but passwords feel a little like doing your homework. You probably don't enjoy homework while you're doing it because you could be doing so many more fun things instead. But you also know that until the experts figure out this whole osmosis thing, old-fashioned studying is the only way to learn. I hope you made it to the end of this chapter not because it was your "homework" but because you wanted to shore up your security by the best means currently available. Passwords are a part of every digital life. Now I have only one question for you? Have you put the book down and changed a password yet?

 ## POP QUIZ:

What's the best way to secure a weak password like "monkey123"?

A. Add an uppercase numeral and a special character, such as $.

B. Don't reuse it anywhere else or share it with anyone.

C. Enable two-factor authentication.

CHAPTER 7

Virtual Peace of Mind

You're being followed—at least you think you are. Every time you take your car out for a spin, you have the distinct impression someone is tailing you to the store, the gym, or your friend's house. Actually, anyone can plainly see you, your car, and your destination if they observe your daily driving routes and patterns because you're on public roads. Now imagine your car plastered with bumper stickers and door signs advertising your home address and your destination as you drive along the same public roads. You're not driving illegally or to some restricted destination, so what's the harm?

Well, just because you have nothing to hide does not mean other people on or off the roads don't have their own agendas. Since anyone can see you and know where you live, they can also know when you're not home. They can track your driving habits and patterns and sell that information to billboard advertisers, police checkpoints, and even thieves. At this point, you might be a little concerned or simply freaked out like me, but there is hope.

A new, Uber-like car service has just arrived and offers fast and easy pickup from anywhere using autonomous vehicles with fully tinted windows for complete privacy. You can now get around town in a different car every day, and no one knows who you are, where you came from, or where you are going. And since you are not the owner of the car, you can park and drive anywhere, even to places that would not allow you access before. Your car is acting as a sort of passport, allowing you to access private roads, park in reserved spaces, and even travel in HOV lanes all day without any other passengers in the car with you. Your newfound privacy on the road makes you feel not only safer but also part of a club with exclusive benefits—but it's not all upside.

Since your autonomous car does the driving, it decides your travel speed, and it's usually slower than most other cars on the road. And it turns out that some businesses do not allow your car to enter their perimeter without paying a small fee because they have a competing service for their own customers. Other car services out there allow you to go anywhere without paying an extra fee, but you'll have to do some research to determine which ones get you to the places you want to go. And speaking of research, none of these new car services are transparent when it comes to the fine print. It's hard to get a straight answer from most as to where they can take you and other terms of services.

There's one more major downside to this new privacy-focused car service: the cost. Of course, it's not free, but it could be free if you're willing to give up one small thing. You can get a free ride every day, providing you let the car service sell your data to retailers, advertisers, and any lawful authority that asks for it. Oh, and you also have to watch their ads anytime you ride in their cars. Those restrictions definitely reduce the privacy benefits you had with the paid car service, but it's a tradeoff some are willing to make.

VIRTUAL PRIVATE NETWORKS (VPNS)

By now, my analogy has probably grown painfully obvious, but if you're still not sure what I'm going on about, I'll spill the beans. Virtual private networks (VPNs) are hugely popular to a variety of different customers for many reasons. A VPN uses a proxy IP address that masks your network from everyone on the internet. VPNs also encrypt your internet browsing, downloads, emails, and most streaming services so that even if a hacker tapped into your network, they couldn't see any discernible data. This assures privacy and a degree of security—particularly for valuable financial or IP data coming directly from your business, personal home network, or even a remote work network connection.

Anyone can set up a VPN to work with existing internet service providers (ISPs), but not all VPNs are created equal.

If you value your privacy at all, the general rule is to stay away from all *free* VPN services. Free VPNs monetize their services by selling your activity to advertisers, and they allow your ISP to see your activity by using weaker data encryption. All VPNs have the encryption keys because they have applied that encryption in the first place. So there is always an element of trust when dealing with any VPN.

In the case of free VPNs, you can expect a steady stream of ads based on your browsing, like from any browser with cookies enabled. Unlike the widely used browser and big data companies, VPNs are *not* subject to nearly as many regulations. Many free VPNs can be rather obtuse in disclosing their terms and conditions. All VPN providers log and encrypt (using their own encryption keys) user data for internal analysis, but the degree to which they protect and share that data is what distinguishes the good ones from untrustworthy ones. While any VPN should hand over data to law enforcement authorities when a legal request is issued, some are quick to comply with government agencies that overstep their authority.[17] Other VPNs even go so far as to deploy malware onto their customers' networks or devices. Free VPNs are usually looking for ways to monetize their services, but surreptitiously installing malware or adware opens up their customers to all kinds of hackers. For all of these reasons, just avoid any free VPN service. Whenever a web company offers a free service, you should assume

---

17   Chris Duckett, "A VPN Will Not Save You from Government Surveillance," ZDNet, April 30, 2017, https://www.zdnet.com/article/a-vpn-will-not-save-you-from-government-surveillance/.

they are selling your web browsing habits to those looking to target you with ads.

DO YOUR VPN RESEARCH

Just because you pay a monthly or onetime fee for a VPN does not mean you can be carefree either. Very few paid or free VPNs have regular external security audits to ensure their customers are getting what they signed up for. Cloak, a ten-dollar-per-month VPN service, is a rare exception that I recommend because they have already undergone a security audit and announced plans to participate in future audits. This bodes well for its customer service, but very few VPNs can make the same claims. Due diligence by researching customer ratings and reviews is a must for anyone shopping for VPNs.

Also be sure to Google the potential VPN for news stories involving responses to data requests by any other companies or authorities. This especially applies to any VPN located outside the United States and subject to another country's laws. It might not matter much to the average consumer looking to stream foreign content that Netflix won't deliver to their country, but political refugees and journalists who need access to content or contacts in China would never use a Chinese-run VPN for fear the country could force the company to hand over all logs and data in order to prosecute them. After all, Chinese IP addresses used by VPNs are among the most valued in the world because a VPN can offer IP addresses only from a country in which its servers are physically located, and many individuals require the complete and uncensored internet for their work while living in or visiting China. VPNs aside, China has been most effective in shutting out the Western world's views via the internet and has truly earned the title of "The Great Firewall."

If you're at all familiar with the Dark Web, you're also familiar with the Tor browser. This browser anonymizes Dark Web browsing from almost everyone except skilled hackers who can exploit the Tor entry node. But this common attack method is thwarted by the additional encryption layer VPNs provide, so I recommend everyone use a trusted VPN in conjunction with Tor browsing for any visit to the Dark Web. Not only will hackers and government agencies not be able to identify you, but your own ISP will not even know you are connecting to Tor or the Dark Web if you use a VPN.

REMOTE ACCESS

Business owners also see the real value of VPNs for employees' remote access to the company's network. Virtual private networks are ideal for home office security and simple for traveling employees. When companies utilize a VPN, they allow remote users secured access to their corporate networks with unique identification methods, such as tokens and passwords. VPNs are also handy for mobile devices looking for an anonymous connection to public Wi-Fi. Hackers who have launched man-in-the-middle (MITM) attacks might be sitting in between your device and its internet connection, but all data passing by is encrypted and unreadable to them. MITM means using false digital credentials or certificates to fool a device or user into thinking it is communicating directly with the intended site by rerouting internet traffic through another server.

Regardless of the additional cost and some speed connectivity issues, I can recommend some VPN services for any small business and even personal internet connectivity for certain users. My top VPN providers are:

- PureVPN: 300,000 IP addresses, 2,000+ servers, affordable at $10.95/month, accepts Bitcoin.

- ExpressVPN: 15,000 IP addresses, over 1,700 servers, $6.67/month, accepts Bitcoin.

- NordVPN: 5,000 IP addresses, over 5,000 servers, $11.95/month.

A trusted VPN service offers privacy, security, and encryption that no business can afford to do without. Typical VPNs cost about ten dollars a month, which is only a small additional cost over your ISP bill but a huge benefit to your peace of mind.

 POP QUIZ:
When using a VPN, what's the one thing you cannot hide from ISPs, hackers, and the government?

A. The fact that you're using a VPN.

B. Your identity.

C. Your data.

CHAPTER 8

Minimize Your Digital Footprints

Next time you stroll down a sandy beach, take a moment to glance back at your winding trail of footprints. Do you know that footprints are actually a good means of unique authentication for every person? Now I'm *not* proposing we take off our socks at every TSA security checkpoint, but I want to convey how unique our biometric attributes are and also how difficult it can be to hide or minimize them. If only our digital footprints would disappear as easily as our real ones dissolve when the waves hit the sand. Learning how to minimize our digital footprints will not only save us a lot of time but also prevent security nightmares.

METADATA

When you go online, there is always a unique set of digital footprints left behind. This individualized identity is based on user behavior, data exchanges, and something called "metadata," which is the container around the important data. *Merriam-Webster* defines metadata as "data that provides information about other data."

One popular delivery method of metadata is browser cookies. Cookies simply allow your browser to track your activity within a given website and across many other websites. This explains why you do not need to repeatedly login and set preferences for every website you visit, but cookies are also responsible for why you see ads for items you were just recently shopping for. Cookies are a convenient and powerful way to track users' browsing behavior on almost any device, but they are more limited on mobile devices due to the nature of mobile browsers and app platforms. Nevertheless, cookies and several other browser tracking methods[18] have become a focal point under EU General Data Protection Regulation (GDPR).

GDPR began as an EU initiative to protect user privacy but has been reluctantly adopted by many countries

---

18   Most mobile browsers accept first-party cookies (must be same domain where cookie was first initiated) but generally not third-party cookies. However, alternate methods have been developed for mobile browser tracking, such as Client/Device Generated Identifier, Statistical ID, HTML5 Cookie Tracking, and Universal Login Tracking.

outside of the EU, including the United States. If you've noticed an uptick in annoying cookie warning pop-up windows and messages during recent visits to websites, blame that on GDPR, which was forced on non-EU organizations as of May 2018. Websites don't technically require metadata like cookies, but users have become so accustomed to the convenience that they seldom turn off or delete cookies. Imagine if there was a way never to forget to delete your cookies after each search result but still enjoy the convenience of searching across the internet? DuckDuckGo, a free privacy-focused browser, effectively does this by actively blocking companies like Google and Facebook from tracking users across the web.

When you snap a picture on your phone, you may care only about the picture itself, but that's only half of the story. Every picture includes a unique time stamp, geo-location data, camera settings, file format, and possibly more, depending on the hardware and software used to take that picture. In fact, metadata is so important, it has been used successfully to aid in the conviction or exoneration of suspects in murder trials.

Metadata is also coveted by organizations like the National Security Agency (NSA) and the FBI to prevent cybercrime and global terrorism. Forget clandestine calls and secret meetings; if an agency can determine the time, whereabouts, and associates of a suspected terrorist, it doesn't need to read emails or texts or wiretap phone calls. The metadata generally provides enough actionable information to grant warrants and send in agents to take down the suspects.

According to the *New York Times*, the NSA has recently tripled its data collection from compliant US telecom companies.[19] These companies are not handing over the substance of every phone conversation and text message but rather the logs of those calls and messages. The density of *all* data is too much for even the most sophisticated AI (assisted by agents or is it the other way around?) to comb through in a timely manner, but the logs do provide connection times and places between persons of interest that prove very useful to agents searching for actionable data. Obtaining and searching through these logs is a trivial technical challenge and evades most human rights and privacy watchdog groups due to its limited purview.

METADATA AND SMALL BUSINESSES

So how does metadata apply to you or your small business? You might not worry about government agents tracking your every move, but there are plenty of other bad actors that stand to gain something by tracking you. Social media excels at sharing pictures, opinions, and news with friends and family. But what happens when strangers pose as acquaintances—or worse, we let strangers into our own social network circles? Accidentally sharing your company's confidential IP on a social network that is primarily designed for family and friends is much easier than you might think. In fact, it's as simple as a "like."

---

19   Charlie Savage, "N.S.A. Triples Collection of Data From U.S. Phone Companies," *New York Times*, May 4, 2018, https://www.nytimes.com/2018/05/04/us/politics/nsa-surveillance-2017-annual-report.html.

The most pervasive tracking and data collection tool in the world is Facebook's ubiquitous thumb-up "like" button. Every single day, Facebook's collective 2.3 billion users rack up more than 5.7 billion likes.[20] Likes seem harmless as a single point of data, but like all metadata, there are millions of associated data points that can accompany every like, including whose comment was liked, time of day, whose page the like took place on, and every single word contained within that liked comment. All of these associations are parsed and categorized so that Facebook advertisers can not only identify user preferences but also shape those behaviors for something called "behavioral futures markets," a term coined in the book entitled *The Age of Surveillance Capitalism* by Shoshana Zuboff.[21]

Like the stock market, behavioral futures markets are data sets that are bought and sold by advertisers in an effort to appeal to consumers. However, given the emotional manipulation social networks are capable of, these behavioral markets go one step further by actually "programming" user preferences rather than just observing and collecting them. This essentially signals the end of capitalism and free market trade as we know it.

Only Facebook can sort through all of this data on such an amazingly granular level, but any Facebook user can also see public likes, comments, images, and time stamps. So it's very important that you understand the privacy settings

---

20   Brandwatch, "53 Incredible Facebook Statistic and Facts," January 5, 2019, https://www.brandwatch.com/blog/facebook-statistics/.

21   Shoshana Zuboff, *The Age of Surveillance Capitalism: The Fight For a Human Future at the New Frontier of Power*, (New York: Hachette Book Group, 2019).

and policies of every social network you're using. When you stop using Facebook, your profile continues to live on long after the last time you checked in. In fact, according to a University of Oxford Internet Institute research paper published in April 2019, the dead could outnumber the living on Facebook within the next fifty years.[22]

All companies need clearly outlined and easy-to-understand privacy policies for employees and customers to respect and follow. These privacy and security issues become especially prescient when users begin to share their personal and professional data among multiple accounts or social networks.

BYOD POLICIES AND RELATED ISSUES

Bring your own device (BYOD) policies are hugely popular because they save companies billions of dollars in additional capital expenditures. But every cost-saving measure or convenience has a price, and BYOD's cost comes in the form of security. Employees juggling between personal and professional social accounts, texts, camera rolls, etc. on a single device must adhere to the same security measures for all activity on that device regardless of the content or intent.

Imagine a hacker gains access to an employee's PC or smartphone, perhaps through a phishing email that placed malware allowing remote access. You might find yourself near a Starbucks, trying to connect to Wi-Fi in

---

22   Rachel E. Greenspan, "On Facebook, the Dead Will Eventually Outnumber the Living. What Does That Mean for Our Histories?" *Time*, April 30, 2019, http://time.com/5579737/facebook-dead-living/.

order to send a large video to a friend, but the hacker doesn't care about your videos. The hacker only wants you to connect your smartphone—the same one you bring to your office every day—to their spoofed "Starbucks Wi-Fi access point." Once connected, the hacker can peruse through your files or surreptitiously install malware to remotely connect to your phone at another time. If you don't believe this is happening, just watch a few *Mr. Robot* episodes on the USA Network.

From there, a typical hacker would likely review your search history and employee browsing habits—a quick way to form a small piece of the puzzle when targeting a corporation. Geo-location data will tell the hacker where the company is located and possibly even the area of the building where you spend most of your time. This can be useful for physical break-ins or to place malware directly onto the local PC network for monitoring and collecting login credentials. If the hacker targets a senior executive or a privileged user with administrative access, the risk level to the company is only further magnified.

APPS, THE CLOUD, AND SECURITY

The permanence of digital footprints extends far beyond our devices. Most photo applications, whether they are included or third-party apps we've installed, save all photos to their servers in the cloud. These servers may exist in your country, but due to redundancy, backups, and your country's own data storage laws, they may also reside just about anywhere in the world, including underground, within mountains, and even at the bottom of the ocean, as is the case with Microsoft's research project to determine the feasibility of undersea data storage, Project Natick.

Cloud storage offers so many technological benefits that even privacy-motivated companies like Apple have data centers all across the United States and even in China. Apple claims that only accounts registered in mainland China will be run by a Chinese state-owned company, but that does little to ease customers worried about security and privacy infractions.

In early 2016, Apple's very public fight with the FBI included a multitude of both facts and allegations emanating from all sides. The details are covered in a later chapter, but one of the main takeaways for security- and privacy-minded folks is that anything stored on the cloud is not truly safe. When presented with a court-ordered warrant, most companies, including Apple, generally comply with law enforcement. This means that for all of their marketing promises, all US companies eventually fall in line with every legal request. However, the awkward position some tech companies have had to endure has also led to a solution resembling a lock without a key.

HARDWARE ENCRYPTION

When enforced from end to end, the latest in hardware-encryption standards cannot be broken if residing on only one device. That is to say, unless the owner of that device shares their passcode or willingly unlocks their device with their own unique biometric identifier, no one can decrypt and access their data, including the world's greatest hackers, supercomputers, and government mandates. That is because devices like iPhones include separate hardware circuitry dedicated only to storing and authenticating user data, so that they cannot be compromised through malware or any other software-based attacks. Of course, passcodes can be guessed, but long and strong ones take years to crack, and after ten wrong guesses, the device can be set to erase itself entirely.

To date, only Apple (first appearing in iPhone 5S in 2013), Samsung (first appearing in Galaxy S4 in 2013), and Blackberry (first appearing in Blackberry 10 in 2013) have released specialized security hardware on specific devices for the consumer market. However, Samsung's Knox and Blackberry's Balance are more of a virtualized partition between consumer and business data and suffer from vulnerabilities detected by security experts. All major device manufacturers and operating systems, including the Android L since 2014, have featured full end-to-end encryption, but not all enable this encryption by default. That is why it's always important to support platforms and apps that do not exploit our digital footprints. If you are not overly concerned about your data being used to sell you products based on your search history, be sure you are at least aware of your privacy options when choosing hardware and software.

PRIVACY VIOLATIONS AND TRAVELERS

Consumers and small business owners aren't the only ones who should be concerned with privacy and security. What happens when both the First and Fourth Amendments of the US Constitution are violated in a single border crossing?

In 2017, US customs officers searched an estimated 30,200 cell phones, computers, and other electronic devices at all US borders and airports, a 60 percent increase over the previous year. Since over three hundred million travelers arrive in the United States every year, these border inspections must be carried out at the custom agents' discretions and with no warrants. Many of the travelers include journalists, political refugees, and foreign visitors. Journalists, in particular, undergo intense scrutiny and not just for potential hidden bombs or weapons. The devices journalists regularly use contain confidential sources, witnesses, subjects, and all sorts of investigative data that is seized and copied by customs officials daily. If a reporter refuses to unlock or hand over a device, they are subject to hours of interrogations and even imprisonment.

JOURNALISTS
This border activity is in direct violation of not only the right to privacy but the freedom of speech and freedom of press as well. If journalists cannot maintain the secrecy of their sources, they cannot effectively report on corruption and abuses of power those sources corroborate. This effectively removes an important check that has been in place in the democratic system since its inception. As of early February 2018, the US Department of Homeland Security, US Customs and Border Protection, and US Immigration and Customs Enforcement agencies have argued for a Massachusetts federal district court to dismiss a lawsuit challenging the constitutionality of warrantless search and seizure of devices at the border.

Of course, those protections work both ways. Record numbers of journalists have been murdered and imprisoned in countries like Mexico, Myanmar, and Turkey in recent years. The same government that demands encryption keys and special access to confidential data must share it with the rest of the world, because that is what happens when you force decryption and install backdoors on any device: a vacuum for hackers, foreign states, and law enforcement has been created to move in and confiscate.

In the meantime, journalists both frustrated and afraid for their lives have begun to use burners, or disposable phones, more often. They store, encrypt, and hide only the most vital data elsewhere and simply dispose of the cheap phones before crossing the border.

Other media professionals have turned to password managers and clever implementations, such as 1Password's Travel Mode. In the Travel Mode app, users organize their passwords and data in various vaults according to their value. Travelers are not legally required to provide passwords to border agents, but all devices may be inspected and accessed through other means. Travel Mode allows travelers to provide a password that unlocks only vaults containing less sensitive information. The other more secretive data is encrypted and stored off the device until the user has crossed the border and turned off Travel Mode again. This is not only a great way for reporters to protect valuable data from authorities but also to minimize their digital footprints as they hop between borders.

CONSUMERS

But we're not all international travelers chasing down a hot story for our readers and viewers. Most travelers and technology users are merely consumers trying to live their lives, do their jobs, and raise their families. Perhaps these examples of rights and violations are reserved only for techno-political arguments involving Big Brother and slippery slopes. One of the most frequent questions cybersecurity experts are asked is, "If I'm doing nothing illegal, then why shouldn't I just comply and share all my data with authorities?" This question can quickly become a philosophical argument, so I will try to address it briefly.

Besides the rights guaranteed by the US Constitution for not only US citizens but all legal and illegal foreign visitors, a basic set of similar inalienable human rights exist in most other democratic republics. Here in the United States, you have the right not to incriminate yourself, to protect your privacy, to freedom of speech and assembly, etc. In other instances, you also have the right to protest, refuse, or deny access to your own private thoughts and privacy. Never has a technology converged so strongly with our own unique personalities, associates, and habits as the modern smartphone does.

When it comes to data storage and recall, smartphones are akin to writing the code to the fire safe in your home, memorizing it, and then burning all physical evidence of that code. Law enforcement agents would have us believe they should be allowed to access that code even though it no longer exists in the physical realm. Someday in the near future, the US Supreme Court may be forced to rule on the relationship each of us has with our personal technology. Many of these questions will be addressed, and some will be answered to the chagrin of privacy advocates or law enforcement; both sides will never be content with the verdict. But since we are living in the present, I can only tell you that things are happening. Laws are changing. Attitudes are adjusting. What was perfectly legal last year may not be legal this year.

GOVERNMENT AND CYBER PRIVACY

Do you trust your government? Let's assume you generally do, but do you trust your government when it has access to your personal, private information even with a legal warrant? This same data can incriminate you one year and exonerate you the next. Earlier, we discussed journalists traveling to and from international destinations, but what about immigrants? They have been invited to participate and prosper in the United States and many European nations for centuries. However, as I write this book, borders are closing and walls are being erected in the name of security. Whether you agree with the reasoning behind it or not, is it fair for any individual to be punished for legal acts from their past that are now deemed illegal? Our digital devices are full of these would-be criminal instances; we just don't know which ones are crimes yet. Unfortunately for illegal immigrants, they are quickly learning they may have fallen onto the wrong side of the law these days. Their digital footprints could send them to jail or back to their country of origin. Where will your digital footprints send you?

DIGITAL PHOTOS

Digital footprints aren't just passwords and secret data. According to an InfoTrends estimate, 1.2 trillion digital photos were taken in 2017 alone.[23] It further reports that more than 4.7 trillion digital photos are stored on hard drives and servers. Now keep in mind that we don't always get permission for others to take digital photographs of us. Perhaps we are in the background or do not even realize someone snapped a photo of us—an unintentional photobomb, if you will. Looking beyond the digital photo itself, we can learn a lot about the people in it. As I wrote about metadata earlier, modern digital cameras and smartphones have location data embedded in them by default, but you can hide this data while still allowing the photo to be seen by others.

If you are a Windows user, right-clicking on the image file and selecting "Properties" followed by "Details" tab will display the latitude and longitude of every image. Apple users can right-click on the image file and select "Get Info" followed by "More Info" to see the geo-stamps on each of their images. Of course, you can always elect to turn off the GPS metadata in your smartphone camera, but this must be done *before* the photo is taken. If you don't, the geo-data is entered directly into Google Maps or Facebook, for example, identifying the exact time and place of a person who happened to walk by in the background whether they

---

23   Ed Lee, "Our Best Photos Deserve to Be Printed," InfoTrends, August 12, 2018, https://blog.infotrends.com/our-best-photos-deserve-to-be-printed/.

were tagged in the photo or not.[24] No matter how much Facebook proclaims they're about user privacy, they're not, because it flies in the face of their own business model, which is to collect as much data possible about its users by connecting as many users as possible. If you are that person and you do not want others to know where or when a photo was taken, simply import your photo into any standard photo editor and export with the metadata turned off. But what happens when you did not even take a photo and have no access to it? How do we control our digital footprints when someone else is behind the camera?

GOOGLE STREET VIEW

Google Street View is a hugely popular and convenient way to see places before even visiting them. These places aren't necessarily tourist attractions. They can simply be destinations, such as seeing a new workout gym in an unfamiliar neighborhood before visiting. In order to map millions of streets, homes, and even pedestrians, Google has deployed hundreds of vehicles around the world to achieve this impressive feat. But all of these little conveniences can also add up to privacy issues. Thieves and even hackers can get a clear view of your home, business, and neighborhood before they dumpster dive or find the most vulnerable first-floor window for illegal entry.

I recommend that anyone concerned with privacy should opt out of Google Street View by reporting the issue

---

24   James Vincent, "Facebook's Facial Recognition Now Looks for You in Photos You're Not Tagged in," The Verge, December 19, 2017, https://www.theverge.com/2017/12/19/16794660/facebook-facial-recognition-tagging-photos.

to Google. This procedure works for street address numbers visible in street view, faces of pedestrians, and even license plates. Simply find the area of concern within Google's Street View and choose "Report a Problem." A red rectangle appears, allowing you to adjust the image until only the area of concern is surrounded by that rectangle. Below that image, you can choose the item you want blurred, explain why you want it blurred, and include additional information. I've opted to block out everything, so my house comes up on Google Street View as one big blur.

PRIVACY FOR ACTIONS

Google provides tools allowing us to shield our possessions and ourselves from the public internet, but what about things we might have done? How can digital footprints ever be washed away if giant search engines like Google do not allow the waves to even hit the beach? The "right to be forgotten movement" has been stirring for over a decade. Many European countries that distrust big corporations are successfully fighting back. Citizens who have paid their debt to society or been publicly humiliated do not want the world to be reminded of their past indiscretions. Yet the internet is built on a system of links that are catalogued by search engines, so some people can never truly rid themselves of their past mistakes.

International citizens continue to argue against specific web pages and links as irrelevant or inadequate and go further to suggest that IPs from any country can be easily spoofed, allowing access to all. Search engine giants like Google counter that while countries should be allowed to control their own internet presence, those seeking to extend their reach to other countries or continents would be hindering freedom of speech to all. The European Court of Justice is set to rule on this landmark case in the near future.

SOCIAL MEDIA HACKING

A University of Phoenix study found that "Nearly two in three U.S. adults who have media profiles say they are aware that their accounts have been hacked, and 86% agree they limit the personal information they post due to the fear of it being accessed by hackers."[25] If you need to keep in touch with friends and family or your job requires the use of social media, you can take some proactive steps to keep your digital footprints from getting away from you. Choose only services that allow two-factor authentication (2FA) and then activate it. If your login credentials are ever compromised, the additional step of requiring physical access to another device such as your smartphone will further protect you. This added layer of security can be a nuisance at times but will minimize the chance of your social media account being hacked.

In my first book, I shared the frustration of having my Twitter account hacked, and I subsequently doubled down on long and strong passwords. I have been criticized for writing key passwords in my little black book, but I have never had a single password compromised since adopting this technique. I like to think of my small booklet as a "second

---

25   UOPX News, "Nearly Two-Thirds of U.S. Adults with Social Media Accounts Say They Have Been Hacked," University of Phoenix, April 27, 2016, https://www.phoenix.edu/news/releases/2016/04/uopx-social-media-hacking.html.

factor" because it physically prevents all hackers from gaining access to any passwords or accounts contained within. So long as I keep my book hidden, its effectiveness is matched only by the peace of mind it offers. This technique is also known as "security through obscurity," and while it serves as an added layer of security, it does not prevent anyone from stealing my passwords if they were ever to locate and steal my book. It's the physical layer of separation between the hackers and me that offers true peace of mind. It is why, in most cybersecurity circles, security through obscurity is regarded as a weak defense when compared to encryption and strong passwords and why many turn to password managers instead of pen and paper.

I also use Dashlane, a popular password manager for passwords that are not as critical to my immediate privacy and security. Like all password managers, Dashlane's convenience outweighs its ability to provide absolute security. That is because no password managers are absolute in their security. Some are more susceptible to hacks in the cloud or locally than others, but when it comes to organizational, timesaving security, particularly for frequent travelers like me, password managers cannot be beat. Just make sure your password manager offers a choice of local or cloud storage using a master password that only you know. Password services that rely solely on the cloud are inherently unsecure and more prone to large-scale attacks by hackers.

POP QUIZ:

The best way to minimize your digital footprint is to:

A. Take fewer photos with your smartphone.

B. Travel less with your smartphone.

C. Post less on social media.

CHAPTER 9

DIGITAL SPRING CLEANING

Many enjoy a thorough spring-cleaning as the weather gets warmer. I also recommend a digital cleaning to take inventory of all your accounts and services. List every one you've signed up for and either use or no longer use. Have you ever signed up for Facebook, Instagram, Twitter, Pinterest, LinkedIn, Tumblr, Snapchat, etc.? Ask yourself when you last used them. If it has been longer than six months, I usually delete my profile. Since I regularly change my login credentials every six months anyway, I don't find this exercise excessive. Next, take a moment to search for your name in Google or Bing. If you find old profiles, accounts, or other information you do not want made public, you can request any search engine to delete old entries.

Many users have created Gmail or Yahoo email accounts simply because they were among the first to offer free email plans with plenty of storage over a decade ago. After years of neglect, you might find thousands of old newsletters, offers, and spam collecting digital dust in your inbox that need to be removed. You may not be currently paying for any of these accounts, but that doesn't mean they don't have a great deal of value to marketers or even hackers.

Finally, complete a digital audit of all apps, devices, and website privileges you have given to your various social media accounts and browsers. This one never ceases to amaze the more fervent social media sharers because it's so easy for them to accumulate and then forget about all those single use services or plug-ins. Every website or network is a little different, but usually the first step is to navigate to the "Settings." From there, you will typically see something like "Apps and devices" (Twitter) or "Apps and Websites" (Facebook) or "Extensions" (Google Chrome). If this is the first time you've ever explored your list of past permissions, you might be surprised by how many have piled up over the years. Purge your digital life by removing all those unnecessary permissions. You will sleep easier knowing that hackers and marketers now have fewer ways to transgress your digital space, and with less overhead, you might even notice your browser speed increase.

PROTECTING YOUR DATA

Any self-respecting internet user has made at least a few online purchases. Some even make dozens of online purchases daily. Therefore, it is important to understand the relationship we have with our own data and the relationship we are allowing online retailers and marketers to have with that same data. Many falsely claim that Google, Amazon, and Facebook are selling our data to the highest bidder. As unscrupulous as I might think Facebook is, I do not truly believe they are selling my purchases, likes, habits, and comments to advertisers, but end results can sometimes feel the same.

All legitimate online retailers create a layer of monetization that obscures our personal data from advertisers while still generating the most revenue possible for themselves. It might not feel like it sometimes, but it's in Google's best interest to protect their users' identities and data from advertising vultures. If they didn't, advertisers would directly target each of us, completely bypassing Google's outreach efforts and its business model in the process. But if you follow the money, it always points to every company's motives.

Google is an advertising company. Apple and Microsoft are hardware and services companies. Amazon is an intermediary transaction company. Facebook and Twitter are media companies. They call themselves tech companies, but tech doesn't pay the bills and post huge quarterly profits. Aside from turning off your cookies, I have no useful security tips to offer except to remind you that to some, your data is more valuable than your money—and to others, your money is more valuable than your data. Both poisons will eventually kill you, but you have to pick at least one if you want a place in this technology revolution.

MESSAGING PLATFORMS AND YOUR MOBILE NUMBER

Have you ever had someone you just met ask you for your mobile phone number? It can be an awkward exchange, especially if you are like me. I have been besieged by marketing calls to the point of not answering my phone anymore unless I recognize the caller. I suspect I am not alone in protecting my number, and yet over 1 billion active Facebook Messenger users willingly provided their mobile phone number just to use the service. Purchased by Facebook in 2014 for $19.3 billion, WhatsApp has tied the Facebook Messenger app for the most users in the world. Each service claims over 1.5 billion active users, but since they are both owned by Facebook, it's more like a conglomerate. Like Google's Allo messaging app, Messenger and WhatsApp both feature end-to-end encryption based on Open Whisper Systems technology, but they also do not have encryption enabled by default.

As a result, until users turn on encryption, critics like Edward Snowden will continue to rail against services that do not truly protect users and even go on to hide and obscure the privacy protections they have built into their own services. In a *Wired* piece from early 2018, security researchers from Ruhr-University Bochum in Germany describe a series of flaws in encrypted messaging apps

Signal, Threema, and WhatsApp.[26] They go on to describe the flaws in Threema and Signal as relatively harmless, but since WhatsApp servers control the limits, hackers or even legal government requests would allow access to supposedly private conversations. Even without a breach, when you use a messaging service without end-to-end encryption enabled, Google and Facebook are mining all of your messages in order to inject their own ads and bot services back to you. Perhaps this explains the sharp rise in robocalls.

Most messaging apps require your phone number and request access to your contact list when you initially download the app. Last year, an interesting messaging app called Squealock came onto my radar. Squealock is unique because it does *not* require your mobile phone number. The app uses end-to-end encryption, and you only need to create a unique user ID that can be changed at anytime.

Messaging apps are simply an extension of social networks, so they basically exist to scrape as many contacts from your digital address book as possible; then all of them are given back to the social network in order to monetize all of those contacts through mass advertising. It's insidious. Emails can be created instantly and for free, so they are not nearly as valuable as a real telephone number. Billions of marketing dollars and countless hours have been spent on a single interaction between new users and a new social network account. This single interaction is

---

26   Andy Greenberg, "WhatsApp Security Flaws Could Allow Snoops to Slide into Group Chats," *Wired*, January 10, 2018, https://www.wired.com/story/whatsapp-security-flaws-encryption-group-chats/.

the moment you download a new social app that asks for permission to connect with your contacts. By making this request appear as effortless and benign as possible, social media and messaging apps manage to collectively scrape billions of contacts every year. Names, emails, addresses, and phone numbers hold different values to advertisers, depending on the nature of their goods and services. It's no wonder even simple flashlight apps have come under scrutiny for privacy invasion.[27]

What possible harm could come from a flashlight app asking for access to your GPS data and all of your contacts? As we've witnessed the fallout from seemingly harmless social media quizzes, it's clear there's a lot of money to be made by invading consumers' privacy. If you ever stumble across one of these single-purpose apps asking for personal data, immediately delete it and report it to the app store or website you downloaded it from.

Secure messaging apps like Dust (formerly Cyber Dust) and Signal are popular, but they also require a phone number to validate your account. Dust's FAQ reads, "Validating your phone number on Cyber Dust is the best way to find friends and to help friends find you. We use a professional and secure validation service to prevent spam and misuse of the application. Validating your phone number also guarantees that other users are not using your personal phone number to find friends. Phone numbers are stored as mathematical representations also known as a hash."

---

27   Tom Fox-Brewster, "Check the Permissions: Android Flashlight Apps Criticized over Privacy," *Guardian*, October 3, 2014, https://www.theguardian.com/technology/2014/oct/03/android-flashlight-apps-permissions-privacy.

Since they still use a third-party validation service, phone numbers are being stored and are vulnerable to hacks even as hashes (meaning obfuscating data by replacing it with indiscernible data), which are increasingly easy to reverse engineer when outdated algorithms are used to hash. WhatsApp states, "We ask for your phone number because that is how WhatsApp routes chat messages between you and your contacts, similar to how the SMS system would." In WhatsApp, users have no access to your address book unless you share a contact in chat. Of course, that doesn't stop WhatsApp from storing all of your contacts on their own servers in the meantime.

Messaging platforms that destroy read messages after a brief time, like Snapchat, are becoming increasingly popular. They not only provide a unique security "fuse" for true privacy, but they also hide many indiscretions and messages that could come back to haunt users years later. Snapchat has found an audience of users looking for more conversational, stream-of-consciousness messaging that they don't have to worry about later when adding others to the group, applying for a job, or simply looking for a long-term relationship. While Snapchat is dwarfed by competing platforms like Facebook and Instagram, it continues to enjoy growing usage from a primarily younger audience due to its fun filters, but many others also enjoy the convenience and digital storage space savings due to the platform's ephemeral nature. Note that the aforementioned Squealock not only destroys all traces of messages thirty seconds after they are read but even notifies both parties when a screen capture is attempted.

POP QUIZ:

What is most valuable to companies looking to sell you something?

A. Your phone number.

B. Your email address.

C. Your physical address.

CHAPTER 10

Robocalls Have Gone Viral

The funny thing about robocallers is that everyone knows exactly what I'm talking about. Some advanced spam, malware, and hacking concepts have strange names or acronyms and only rarely appear in the wild, so it's a full-time job to educate people on those matters. But robocalls, as they say, have gone viral.

Most hacks and scams work by targeting 1 percent to 10 percent of total users based on information the perpetrators have. You may assume that spammers and hackers have everyone's email addresses, but they do not, and emails represent only a small piece of the larger digital puzzle that is our identity. Even more so than our Social Security numbers, our phone numbers are a direct line to our identity. Most of us—and especially small business owners—have multiple email addresses, bank accounts, and even shipping addresses, but we all have that single mobile phone number to keep in touch with friends and family and receive an occasional emergency phone call.

I speak with thousands of small business owners every year, and every single one of them receives daily robocalls they would like to stop. I don't think anyone feels particularly threatened by robocallers, but they can be a real time suck if you're always inclined to answer your phone. I understand that some millennials and Gen Zers are so busy texting that they have yet to answer or make a voice call on their phones, but I do not have that luxury. I am a middle-aged businessman with a wife and two kids; these facts require voice calls several times a day. Of course, I recognize their phone numbers and all of my contacts appear by name and face on my phone, but I do not know the number of my son's new pediatrician, my wife's carpool coworker, or the new pizza place we decided to give a try, so I must answer.

On an average day, I receive five or six robocalls, and I am not alone. The number-one consumer complaint to the Federal Trade Commission (FTC) and Federal Communications Commission (FCC) is about telemarketing calls. By the end of 2017, it was reported that over 2.4 billion robocalls were placed each and every month.[28] If you do the math, you'll see that these are not infrequent calls but repeated harassment spread across every phone user.

The FTC received 4.5 million complaints about robocalls in 2017 and has begun aggressively combating this growing telephone spam problem with new initiatives.[29] They have even launched the FTC Robocall Challenge by encouraging industry experts and tech gurus to help track down and stop robocallers.[30] The FCC created the Call Blocking Order back in 2017 as a way to assist phone companies in weeding out the robocalls from the real ones to more effectively block them. This obviously never caught on because in 2018, thirty-five attorneys general signed a formal request for the FCC to take action, specifically against "neighbor spoofing" robocalls.[31]

Neighbor spoofing is when an incoming robocall matches the first six digits of your own phone number in the hopes of fooling you into answering the call from someone you might know. Technically, spoofing is legal unless the party on the other end of the line uses it for fraudulent purposes, such as misrepresenting who they are or why they are calling you. Robocallers might be irritating and harassing, but they are usually upfront in what they are selling.

28   Adi Robertson, "Robocalls Were Worse Than Ever in 2017," The Verge, January 1, 2018, https://www.theverge.com/2018/1/1/16837814/robocall-spam-phone-call-increase-2017-ftc-report.

29   Adi Robertson, "Robocalls Were Worse Than Ever in 2017," The Verge, January 1, 2018, https://www.theverge.com/2018/1/1/16837814/robocall-spam-phone-call-increase-2017-ftc-report.

30   Federal Trade Commission, "Robocalls: Humanity Strikes Back," Accessed April 2, 2019, https://www.ftc.gov/news-events/contests/robocalls-humanity-strikes-back.

31   Jennings Brown, "35 States Tell the FCC to Get Off Its Ass and Do Something About Spoofed Robocalls," Gizmodo, October 9, 2018, https://gizmodo.com/35-states-tell-the-fcc-to-get-off-its-ass-and-do-someth-1829637040.

PROACTIVE PREVENTION STEPS

One proactive step you can take is to register your landline or mobile phone number with the National Do Not Call Registry at www.donotcall.gov. There is no cost to register your phone number, and it typically takes about one month for the robocalls to subside. Calls for charities, debt collectors, and political groups will still be allowed to go through. If you continue to receive robocalls after registering, report this to the Federal Trade Commission. Remember that just listing your phone number on the National Do Not Call Registry does not guarantee you won't ever be called. Whenever I've reported to these agencies, I do notice a slight dip in robocalls, but they go back to the same level in a few months.

PHONE SPAM

The similarities between robocalls and spam do not stop just at the annoyance. I treat robocalls just like I treat spam. In other words, if I am not expecting a call, I do not answer and simply let them leave a message. Like social engineering, robocallers are sometimes simply looking to get an affirmation from you. Therefore, never say "Yes" if a robocall asks any question because your entire conversation is being recorded. For example, if the robocaller asks whether you would like to not receive any more calls like this, hang up. If you answer affirmatively, they can use your recorded response as confirmation of your interest in their services. Another common trap you may have heard is when the "caller" asks if you can hear them. If you answer "Yes," your voice signature may be used for future fraudulent purposes.

At least once a day, I peruse my voice mail messages just like I also go through my junk email filter. My iPhone provides me a convenient voice-to-text transcription feature offering instant visual confirmation of spam, but Google's Pixel 3 goes one step further. All Pixel 3 phones offer Google's own call-screening feature that can answer the phone for you, let the caller know you're using a screening service, and then ask them to identify themselves. The cool thing about this feature is that it can all play out in real time so you can screen calls from friends, family, or robocallers and then decide at any time whether you want to pick up the phone. It's old-school answering machine screening brought into the twenty-first century that also allows you to tag the caller as a spammer. Unfortunately, as we all know, spammers cannot be stopped by simply blocking one of their numbers or emails; they will use others and keep at it.

As fruitless as it may be, I do take some small satisfaction from blocking a robocall, but that blocking and screening takes time. Robocalling is all about quickly sifting through potential customers in order to get through to a real one ready to spend money. As soon as you answer a robocall and engage with the automated dialogue, you will be switched over to a live operator. Jolly Roger Telephone Company allows victims to turn the tables on their spammers by using their own robots to create endless dialogue to actually fool live telemarketers. You can even customize your robot's personality. The cost for the service is two dollars a month or six dollars for a one-year subscription, which seems like small price to pay for a little revenge.

THERE'S AN APP FOR THAT

Many customers also complain directly to their phone providers who, in response to potentially losing customers, have developed their own tools to fight back against these pesky robocalls. Carriers have learned to carefully analyze calling patterns on their networks and are working with law enforcement to head off robocalls at the pass. Naturally, phone companies have a conflict of interest, since the robocallers are also their customers, but they have introduced apps that can help. AT&T's free Call Protect app has good reviews in both the App Store and Google Play and claims to "block potential fraud calls." Sprint offers a fraudulent call-blocking app to customers of their My Sprint service, and T-Mobile has recently introduced their own Name ID app to all app stores. Verizon was the last to join the fray when they recently released their free "Call Filter" app that alerts users to likely spam alongside a three-dollar-per-month version that additionally identifies unknown callers and includes tools to look up spam numbers and a robocall risk meter.

There are also third-party party apps that block robocalls so your phone will not ring. These apps deliver an "out-of-service" message to all robocalls. RoboKiller costs $1.99 a month to stop spam calls and even identifies local phone numbers that are being spoofed. Another popular app is Nomorobo, which is also $1.99 per month and has similar features. The app landscape constantly changes, as does the database of spoofed and spam numbers these apps pull from, so it's important to keep an eye out for the latest apps and updates.

Another growing trend you may have noticed is the spontaneous voice mail spam without a ring. Some people just ignore these messages, assuming they were simply experiencing bad coverage during the call, but in fact, they are a new breed of targeted spam calls that go directly to your voice mail without ringing. Fortunately, consumer protection groups have successfully been able to include these calls in the National Do Not Call Registry. It goes without saying that you should never call back any of these missed marketing calls unless you want to guarantee a top spot on their call lists.

THE PRICE OF ROBOCALLS

In my research, I have found robocallers typically paying less than one cent per call for a package of ten thousand robocalls, and this price drops even more for larger packages. It would appear that the best way to fight back is to ignore and not answer any unexpected calls, but this might not be entirely true. The *Wall Street Journal* reported that when you do not answer the phone, many phone companies pay a tiny amount of money (fractions of a penny) back to callers in exchange for a little data on each call they placed.[32] These huge databases are then sold back to marketers and advertisers, some of which are the very same robocallers supplying that data. Clearly, something is wrong with the entire system when robocallers are being partially subsidized for consumer

---

32   Sarah Krouse, "Why Robocallers Win Even if You Don't Answer," *Wall Street Journal,* June 4, 2018, https://www.wsj.com/articles/why-robocallers-win-even-if-you-dont-answer-1528104600.

harassment by the very companies providing phone service to the targeted customers.

In early 2019, FCC Chairman Ajit Pai called on all carriers to implement a national caller ID authentication system by the end of 2019.[33] In his ultimatum to carriers, Pai threatens regulatory action if they do not meet this FCC deadline, but it is unclear exactly how much cooperation or effort is required from all the carriers. The same demand was made to all carriers by the FCC back in late 2018 with very little demonstrated progress. Some carriers have announced plans to roll out their more robust caller ID services already, but others remain silent. Hopefully this time carriers will realize that unsolicited calls are not just a huge waste of time and resources but a violation that must be dealt with as a threat to their customers, just like any form of malware.

 POP QUIZ:
What's the best way to deal with pesky robocalls?

A. Ask to speak with their supervisor.

B. Use a carrier-approved smartphone app.

C. Register your phone number on the National Do Not Call Registry.

33   ACA International, "FCC Chairman: It's Time for Caller ID Authentication Systems," February 14, 2019, https://www.acainternational.org/news/fcc-chairman-its-time-for-caller-id-authentication-systems.

Part 2: An Exclusive Club You Do Not Want to Join

CHAPTER 11

Ashley Madison Is Cheating the Cheaters

Before August 20, 2015, the Ashley Madison website was known by most as a purveyor of lascivious ads and services to facilitate extramarital affairs for its subscribers. The slogan, "Life is short. Have an affair," spoke volumes to the clientele and the simplicity of its service. That all changed when the Impact Team, a group of hackers looking to make a name for themselves, announced their successful hack of Ashley Madison servers and leaked over 25 GB of user data. Some thirty million Ashley Madison accounts were also compromised, but the actual number of users became fuzzy upon further investigation, due in part to the discovery of many thousands of bogus female user accounts. Data analysts found that only roughly twelve thousand of the 5.5 million registered female accounts were used regularly.[34] This discrepancy between genuine and bogus accounts meant that only three out of every one thousand women were legitimate users, painting a very different picture than Ashley Madison presented to its user base. This wouldn't be the last time Ashley Madison was caught engaging in activity counterproductive to its subscribers' expectations.

Security analysts combed through the leaked data and found that passwords were hashed by using SHA1, an algorithm widely known to be vulnerable to rehashing called "bcrypt." Coding errors led to eleven million passwords being cracked using fairly simple password-recovery tools. In a sampling of four thousand of the easiest crackable passwords, "123456" and "password" were the most common. These real-world security weaknesses by both Ashley Madison and its users cannot be overstated.

---

34   Annalee Newitz, "Almost None of the Women in the Ashley Madison Database Ever Used the Site," Gizmodo, August 26, 2015, https://gizmodo.com/almost-none-of-the-women-in-the-ashley-madison-database-1725558944.

PASSWORD HACKING

Since the hacks centered around weak passwords hashed in a weak form, a top ten list of passwords were ranked by popularity and frequency of use for all to see. You just cannot make up this kind of stuff.

RANK	PASSWORD	FREQUENCY
1	123456	900,420
2	12345	635,995
3	123456789	585,150
4	12345678	145,867
5	1234567890	133,414
6	1234567	112,956
7	password	101,046
8	qwerty	86,050
9	qwertyuiop	43,755
10	987654321	40,627

It doesn't take a mathematician to see how often weak passwords are used and how easy it is to simply guess your way into many accounts simply by applying a brute-force login script of the weakest passwords. Likewise, it doesn't take a statistician to understand that reusing weak passwords opens your home or small business to far more attacks than using *different* weak passwords. The typical Ashley Madison user's motives might be questionable, but their security habits are not constrained to the adult-dating website. These all-too-familiar weak passwords have shown up on all kinds of websites from eBay to the Dark Web black markets.

ADULTFRIENDFINDER BREACH

Before I continue, I'd be remiss in not mentioning another huge breach of a competing dating website. Before the dust could even settle on Ashley Madison, AdultFriendFinder admitted to a massive breach involving some 412 million accounts. As the largest dating website, AdultFriendFinder's data went back nearly twenty years and affected many other adult webcam sites, such as iCams.com, Cams.com, Stripshow.com, and Penthouse.com, which are all owned by AdultFriendFinder networks. With so many users and websites under one network breach, user names, zip codes, emails, birth dates, and IP addresses were readily found across the internet.

BITCOIN EXTORTION

Regardless of affiliations with either dating network, users with truly strong passwords were spared the embarrassment their less-security-minded fellow members had to endure. However, many Ashley Madison users were not spared the public humiliation, including twelve hundred Saudi Arabian emails released. Adultery is punishable by death in Saudi Arabia. In addition, several thousand US military and government emails were also revealed. These account holders were immediately targeted for extortion for approximately two hundred Bitcoins to keep their identities secret. The breach sunk to a new level of danger on August 24, when Toronto police announced two suicides directly related to the data leak.[35]

---

35   Sam Thielman, "Toronto Police Report Two Suicides Associated with Ashley Madison Hack," *Guardian*, August 24, 2015, https://www.theguardian.com/world/2015/aug/24/toronto-suicides-ashley-madison-hack.

As it turns out, this giant data breach was only a symptom of a much deeper security problem within Ashley Madison for its parent company, Avid Life Media, which also owned the Cougar Life and Established Men hookup websites. For starters, the email signup on Ashley Madison did not require user email verification to register. This means that anyone could sign up an unsuspecting user without their knowledge or permission. Perhaps someone had a grudge against you, mistyped their own email as yours, or was a friend playing a bad joke on you. It didn't matter, because Ashley Madison created user accounts for millions without any verification required.

DIGITAL BLACKMAIL, SPOUSAL SPYING, AND CORPORATE RISK

Long before the personal data, sexual kinks, and gender preferences of millions of users were leaked to the world, there was also a simple little hack any blackmailer or suspicious spouse could easily perform. Simply log in with the email of the spouse or employer you suspected might be an Ashley Madison member. If that email was not already registered with Ashley Madison, the person would receive a response indicating that the email was not recognized. But if the email was already registered, it would simply reply that the password was not recognized, so the email was already confirmed without even logging in.

Many Ashley Madison members used their work emails, probably in an attempt to keep their spouse or significant other from reading their messages. You may not have dominion over your employees' private dealings, but when they use your company email to sign up for any service, they put your business at risk by exposing the domain to all types of spam, phishing, and malware attacks. Any correspondence originating from your company server becomes a potential liability, just like any correspondence landing on your server is ultimately owned by the company that owns that server.

Be sure to inform your human resources department or individual employees about company policies and their privacy rights when using company computers, emails, or even letterhead. All employees and management must understand that company security will always eclipse employee privacy rights when using company networks on company grounds. Ultimately, this protects much more than just the company.

GOVERNMENT EXPOSURE

Approximately fifteen thousand of the leaked accounts were linked to email addresses with .edu, .mil, or .gov accounts. Therefore, the names and personal information of thousands of government employees are now online, making them a target for blackmail and identity theft. This raises serious public security concerns. With almost two-thirds of the fifteen thousand emails containing military suffixes, blackmail and threats come into play. The US military has regulations against cheating on spouses, and the leak could lead to many dishonorable discharges should the military decide to follow up. In addition, several state and local government agencies stated they will be looking into accounts that used email addresses linked to their employees.

Since Ashley Madison did not require email verification, anyone could sign up for a free account without someone else's consent. Confirming the information is difficult, since neither Ashley Madison nor its cheating users are likely to comment. On the other hand, people who were wrongfully signed up by others have no viable way to prove their innocence either.

PUBLIC SHAMING

Some of the leaked accounts contained enough specific data, such as credit card information, to trace certain individuals; some are undoubtedly legitimate, but others were obviously faked. True to their threats, on August 18, 2015, the Impact Team hacker group posted a giant list of "cheaters" on the Dark Web. The personal details of more than thirty million Ashley Madison users were revealed in that one 9.7 GB file with over 100 GB of other sensitive information harvested by the criminals, including phone numbers, physical addresses, credit card numbers, and even sexual preferences.[36]

This so-called "cheaters list" was immediately scoured by all sorts of anxious visitors, but not all the emails were legitimate, especially ones originating from government jobs. For example, foxmulder@fbi.gov and darth@vader.gov were both discovered, so the list was obviously littered with fakes and jokes, but that is of little consolation to real users who have been outed.

---

36   Krebs on Security, "Who Hacked Ashley Madison?" August 26, 2015, https://krebsonsecurity.com/tag/impact-team/.

CAN CHEATERS PROSPER?

In addition to the public shaming and possible destruction to their marriages, many Ashley Madison users also paid Ashley Madison for a service that purportedly protected their account information by deleting it once the user left the service. Obviously, it didn't work. One of the reasons Ashley Madison became a target in the first place was due to its smug advertisements touting the service's security and discretion. Many users paying for account deletion were included in the hack dumped on the Dark Web. So Ashley Madison not only enabled cheating among its users but also cheated its own users in the process.

In 2016, Avid Life Media was rebranded, officially changing its name to ruby Corp. and ousting CEO Noel Biderman. It's no surprise that such a publicly stained company would want a complete rebranding, but only time will tell if it will be enough.

Since the 2015 hack, ruby Corp. has been forced to pay out only $1.66 million in fines to the FTC, as well as complying with a twenty-year oversight agreement with the agency. This sharply reduced fine was part of an agreement that includes mandatory risk assessments, new security protocols, and system upgrades. The company has begun to pay $17.5 million to the users affected by the breach, with some claims reaching up to $3,500 depending on losses. Unfortunately, the remainder of the settlement has been suspended due to the company's inability to pay.

With so many mistakes and lies on both sides of the firewall, it's hard to sum up the salient security misses in this breach. All of the usual best practices apply, but one stands out in my mind as a clear takeaway. There's been a fair amount of judgment and finger-pointing both within the media and in the public's reaction to the media coverage of the Ashley Madison breach. I want everyone to remember that no one deserves to have their privacy invaded or identity stolen or revealed unless they are posing a true threat or conspiring to threaten others. In those cases, a legally obtained warrant is not only understandable but required. But some seem to think that just because Ashley Madison caters to a lower form of morality that it and its users deserve to be punished by hackers. Hackers might have targeted Ashley Madison for some morally judgmental reasons, but hackers will target anyone for nearly any agenda they claim.

Hacker groups like the Impact Team actively violate the law, hurt many people, and cost millions of dollars. They are not to be confused with a Robin Hood–like agenda, because even the socially motivated ones are still in the game for themselves. If they're not in it for strictly the glory or bragging rights—it's the money or the power. And make no mistake: no one type of user on the internet is more safe than another type of user. Gamers, bankers, consumers, political appointees, executives, philanthropists, small businesses, families, and every-one they know are vulnerable to attack. Only people who regularly adhere to cybersecurity best practices have a chance of avoiding the sting of the hack.

POP QUIZ:
Which organization is most vulnerable to hacking?

A. Charitable organizations with weak cybersecurity.

B. Black market websites with strong cybersecurity.

C. Your business.

CHAPTER 12

Yahoo Has Been Hacked Again and Again

One of the original internet darlings, Yahoo has had more than its share of ups and downs and has successfully reinvented itself numerous times over the past twenty years. Yahoo was originally founded in 1994 by Jerry Yang and David Filo as the "friendlier alternative" to services like AOL or CompuServe. Even its playful name is an acronym for "Yet Another Hierarchically Organized Oracle," so it's just a catalog for managing websites.

When it went public in 1996, Yahoo was valued at $848 million, and that was before the dotcom boom. By 2000, Yahoo was valued at $125 billion. Interestingly, in 2002, Yahoo even put out an unsuccessful bid to acquire a lesser-known upstart called Google for $3 billion. By 2008, the dotcom bubble had long been burst, yet Yahoo turned down a $44.6 billion acquisition deal from Microsoft. At one point, Yahoo was reporting over seven billion views every month and even ran Super Bowl ads, but those days are long gone. Add a few failed IPs like Tumblr, a questionable merger with AOL, and a string of eight different CEOs over its twenty-four-year history, and you have the makings of a great comeback story without the comeback. And this was all setting the stage for Yahoo's greatest failure: the largest known internet hack ever, one so large it would include every single remaining Yahoo account holder.

But before proceeding, I want to clarify some confusion over the actual breaches and the time lines of those breaches. There were actually two separate major data breaches of Yahoo. The first one was disclosed in September 2016 and identified five hundred million compromised accounts. That actual breach occurred sometime in 2013, however. In December 2016, Yahoo acknowledged a second separate breach that actually occurred back in August 2013, involving some one billion more accounts. Then in October 2017, Yahoo affirmed that the one billion accounts were actually three billion accounts, which means every Yahoo account.

DUBIOUS DISTINCTION

In fact, Yahoo is the only company that holds the title for having the two largest data breaches in internet history. While these tremendous numbers are truly concerning, I worry much more about the timelines. Names, phone numbers, birth dates, emails, and more were being traded and sold on the Dark Web unbeknownst to the users, translating into years of inevitable credit fraud, ransomware, and phishing attacks. The part that concerns me—and should concern you too—is that hackers have had access to all of Yahoo's customers for several years, and yet Yahoo has still shared no details as to when it really first knew about this. So the security warnings and password resets arrived years later, long *after* the damage was already done. And there is no telling how long this damage will continue to affect users across the internet.

In a 2016 security notice posted online by former CISO Bob Lord, Yahoo stated: "A recent investigation by Yahoo has confirmed that a copy of certain user account information was stolen from the company's network in late 2014 by what it believes is a state-sponsored actor. The account information may have included names, email addresses, telephone numbers, dates of birth, hashed passwords (the vast majority with bcrypt) and, in some cases, encrypted or unencrypted security questions and answers . . ." It continued: "Based on the ongoing investigation, Yahoo believes that information associated with at least 500 million user accounts was stolen and the investigation has found no evidence that the state-sponsored actor is currently in Yahoo's network. Yahoo is working closely with law enforcement on this matter."

If the passwords were truly hashed, why should that concern any Yahoo users? Because Yahoo used an outdated technique to hash passwords (originally MD5 and then with slightly improved bcrypt hashing) on its site, and it's relatively easy for modern graphic processing units (GPUs) to compromise it. Remember the millions of Ashley Madison user names leaked to the internet? Those were also bcrypt hashes, but not all hashes (not even all bcrypt hashes) are the same. In cryptography, MD5 is a password-hashing function that was once resistant to brute-force attacks, but due to increased computing power that's no longer the case.

Once passwords are "hashed" by scrambling characters into unreadable strings, they must then be "salted" to prevent advanced GPUs from "reverse hashing" by comparing the hash with commonly used passwords. "Salting" introduces random data to further password scrambling. Algorithms like bcrypt dynamically slow the rate at which passwords can be guessed, thereby frustrating most hackers who generally look for the biggest payout quickly. I will return to some more details when discussing cryptocurrency and Bitcoin mining.

Yahoo utilized the MD5 algorithm, a popular hash function that produces a 128-bit value that is neither encrypted nor encoded; it was developed by MIT Professor Ronald Rivest in 1991. It can be cracked by a brute-force attack and has numerous documented vulnerabilities. According to the CMU Software Engineering Institute, the MD5 algorithm has been considered "cryptographically broken and unsuitable for further use" since 2010,[37] yet many companies continue to use it.

A common thread among large breaches is that the scope and size of such exploits are so tremendous and lead to so many unknowns that companies are reluctant to disclose anything. Good hackers leave little to no trace of their presence, so even good cyber forensics teams have difficulty discerning the full extent of a breach, which puts companies in an awkward position. After all, it's much easier to avoid putting your foot in your mouth when you keep your mouth shut. But in the world of cybersecurity, this behavior is not only harmful to everyone involved—except the hackers—it's also illegal.

BREACH NOTIFICATION REQUIREMENTS

Companies need to act swiftly without putting their heads in the sand. Postponing any breach notifications to customers and the public can have devastating effects. Yet Yahoo disclosed the first, smaller breach of five hundred million users a full two years *after* it had occurred. The second major breach, which actually occurred in August 2013, did not get full disclosure until October 2017. It can take months for cyber forensics teams to sort through all the exposed data and security holes to learn the full extent of a hack. Clearly, that is not what happened here, because Yahoo waited years to notify the public and its investors.

We've seen shady timing involving breach announcements by executives looking to cash out their stock before

---

37   Wikipedia, s.v. "MD5," last modified July 6, 2019, https://en.wikipedia.org/wiki/MD5.

the market punishes their payout; the Yahoo situation does not appear to be much different. Except in this case, Yahoo stood to gain billions of acquisition dollars from Verizon by keeping the news quiet. In July 2018, Verizon agreed to buy Yahoo's web assets for $4.83 billion. Sure, that was a mere 0.04 percent of Yahoo's valuation at its highest point, so it could have been viewed as a fire sale, but after Yahoo's collapse at the end of the twentieth century, it did rebound. In 2005, Yahoo spent $1 billion on a 40 percent stake in a lesser-known Chinese company called Alibaba. This investment proved very lucrative, as Alibaba quickly rose to become a $50 billion-dollar competitor to e-commerce behemoth Amazon. By the end of 2017, Alibaba would go onto become a $500 billion company, bolstering Yahoo's value with it along the way.

Meanwhile, Verizon had acquired AOL back in 2015 and had a grand scheme in mind. It planned to merge AOL's many valuable properties—such as TechCrunch, Huffington Post, Engadget, and Moviefone—with Yahoo's Tumblr, Flickr, and Yahoo Sports platforms under one entity called "Oath: a Verizon company." But long before this plan was hatched by Verizon, Yahoo was hacked and hacked again. Once revealed, the breach estimates from Yahoo seemed to rise in sync with the lowering of the company's value. Verizon finally closed its final purchase price of Yahoo for $4.5 billion, a $350 million discount, primarily due to the previously undisclosed breaches.

Security experts predict both breaches could still bring about expensive class action lawsuits, in addition to other costs. The previously mentioned *Ponemon Institute*

2016 Cost of Data Breach Study found that the typical cost to remediate a data breach is $221 per stolen record.[38] Added up, that could top Yahoo's original $4.8 billion sales price by over 138 times or $663 billion, which is more than Alphabet, Microsoft, or Amazon are each worth.

Verizon must be confident in its ability to get a handle on possible fallout from this acquisition. Since taking over as CEO in 2012, Marissa Mayer had nearly doubled Yahoo's value, but that wasn't enough for Verizon. As part of the acquisition details, Mayer stepped down as Yahoo CEO in June 2017. Later that year, she testified before the Senate Commerce Committee on the breach. She claimed that Yahoo did not know of the 2013 breach and learned of it only through intrusion files presented in 2016. Mayer also noted that all companies are effectively in an "arms race" with private hackers and state-sponsored actors as methods "become more sophisticated." I do not believe we will ever uncover a "smoking gun" that reveals Yahoo was downright deceptive or truly negligent, but I think it's safe to assume a little of both.

STATE-SPONSORED HACKS

Meanwhile, Yahoo continues to work closely with law enforcement, but as you might recall, so did J. P. Morgan back in 2015 until the FBI filed charges against them for an insider "pump-and-dump" scheme that led to the arrest of four cyberthieves. That hack was initially tied to Russian

---

38 Larry Ponemon, Ponemon Institute, *Ponemon Institute 2016 Cost of Data Breach Study*, June 16, 2016, https://www.ponemon.org/news-2/23.

gangs and government-sponsored hacks, so Russia appears to have been J. P. Morgan's scapegoat. And four Russians have been officially charged with hacking the five hundred million Yahoo accounts, according to the US Justice Department.[39] Some of the hackers were even reported to have been offering services for compromising email passwords. As of this writing, there is still ongoing investigation as to who is truly behind the three billion Yahoo accounts that were hacked. So where does that leave us?

THE AFTERMATH OF A BREACH

After the dust settles and the news cycle moves onto the next security scandal or major breach, hackers begin the next phase of their dirty work. Hundreds of millions of Yahoo user accounts will continue to receive harmless-looking emails. These are socially engineered attacks looking to collect further personal information from Yahoo users. Targeted emails will be sent out to three billion Yahoo email accounts, warning users to change their passwords immediately. Such emails are carefully crafted by hackers with a step-by-step on how to quickly update passwords, including URLs and fake login screens. Users need only respond to breach headlines by logging into Yahoo directly and changing their password. Unfortunately, when three billion people are targets, many millions will not heed the proper security advice. They may forget to change their

39   Vindu Goel and Eric Lichtblau, "Russian Agents Were Behind Yahoo Hack, U.S. Says," *New York Times*, March 15, 2017, https://www.nytimes.com/2017/03/15/technology/yahoo-hack-indictment.html.

passwords—or worse, fall into the hacker's grasp even further by clicking on links in bogus emails purportedly from Yahoo.

Password reuse is another huge problem. Once a password is compromised, hackers use automated software that attempts logins with that same compromised password across myriad websites. Over 59 percent of Americans reuse the same password across more than one website, and over 95 percent of Americans share up to six passwords with family members.[40] Hackers know these stats and the best ways to exploit them. It might take Yahoo and the feds years to sort through this mess, but you can secure all of your accounts right now.

 POP QUIZ:

When is it OK to reuse a password?

A. When you are logging into social media accounts.

B. When it is too hard to remember a long password.

C. Never.

---

40   Jacob Siegal, "95% of Americans Share Passwords with Friends and Family Members," BGR, February 18, 2016, https://bgr.com/2016/02/18/lastpass-sharing-passwords-security-survey/.

CHAPTER 13

Massive Breach Befitting a Massive Hotel Chain

After covering dozens of major breaches that have affected billions of users, haven't we seen the worst of it? No. On November 30, 2018, I received an email and subsequent phone call from Associated Press radio, asking me to weigh in on the Marriott data breach dominating the headlines that morning. This was news to me, so I jumped on my computer to get up to speed and quickly realized this breach was a biggie. Over the course of four years, five hundred million customers of Marriott and its many sister chains had been affected, although Marriot has since issued an update stating that the number of compromised guests did not break 383 million.

Returning the AP's call was my next order of business for two reasons. First, it's important to always stay "out there" professionally for my listening and viewing public. After years of absorbing and dissecting breaches, I've developed a shorthand for parsing these events in a way that listeners and viewers can more easily digest and, hopefully, remember. Secondly, like with the 2013 Target hack, I was and still am a Marriott customer, so this affected me on a personal level. The story might have gotten trampled by the latest presidential tweet or holiday season super sale, but it wasn't going away for me that easily. As it turned out, the news media felt the same way. Perhaps all of those field reporters staying at Starwood Hotels & Resorts properties over the past four years were feeling the same pangs as me. Later that day, I received two additional interview requests from other news outlets, so the story had legs.

In massive data breaches, the most important question to answer first is *Who?* The scale of this attack and sprawl of Starwood Hotels & Resorts properties would indicate that just about every frequent traveler and many small business owners would be affected. Now let me save you a few minutes of Googling. To give you a clearer picture, take the time to review your own purchases at any of the following additional Marriott/Starwood Hotels & Resorts brand hotels and cancel credit cards if you haven't already:

- W Hotels
- St. Regis, Sheraton Hotels & Resorts
- Westin Hotels & Resorts, Element Hotels
- Aloft Hotels
- The Luxury Collection
- Tribute Portfolio
- Le Méridien Hotels & Resorts
- Four Points by Sheraton

In addition to credit card information, personal information, such as name, address, phone, email, birth dates, and passport numbers for international travelers were also compromised. In fact, some twenty-five million passports in all were compromised, and 5.25 million of them were never even encrypted on Marriot's end. And despite the fact that credit card information was encrypted using the AES-128 standard, Marriott representatives say that they cannot rule out the possibility that hackers also stole decryption keys for all of those credit card numbers. Needless to say, when your credit card, birth date, and passport numbers are packaged together on the Dark Web, their sale can fetch much more money than any credit card number alone. Typical credit card numbers may fetch from three to five dollars each, but a bundle like this may reach ten dollars each. This may not seem like much until you factor in the totality of five hundred million accounts typically bundled together ten thousand at a time. That's $100,000 per Dark Web customer with a possible total take of $5 billion for all of the data! Certainly not chump change by any standards, especially for the Marriott customers like me who unwillingly contributed to these illicit transactions.

THE BREACH DETAILS

You might wonder what specifically happened with the Marriott breach. On September 8, 2018, Marriott's internal security tools alerted them about an attempt to access the Starwood guest reservation database. After contacting leading security experts, Marriott learned that unauthorized access to the Starwood networks went all the way back to 2014. An unauthorized party had apparently copied and encrypted guests' information and took steps to remove their tracks before the hack was ultimately revealed. On November 19, 2018, Marriott decrypted the data and determined the contents were from the Starwood guest reservation database.

Keep in mind that a savvy cyberthief could also glean some additional information from the compromised data, such as customer gender, arrival and departure information, and communication preference. These additional data points might seem benign or even trivial, but consider your travel patterns and the greater implications for your home when you are away. Hackers can use or sell this information to burglars looking for easy scores.

The Marriott breach included payment card account numbers and expiration dates that were encrypted using

Advanced Encryption Standard (AES-128). AES-128 bit is government-level encryption and very difficult to hack. Most cyberthieves know this and would not attempt to decrypt AES-128 bit encryption, but the decryption keys were also reportedly stolen, making the decryption easy. As this breach continues to be investigated, I'm confident we will get more tidbits along with some answers to open questions.

IF YOU'VE BEEN COMPROMISED

So how can you find out whether you are affected, and are there any proactive steps you could take? First, you can look back through your emails for messages from Marriott around late November or early December 2018. The message contains a standard apology and security warning language just like any breach notification, but also know there is a high probability that hackers will initiate phishing attacks through emails that appear to be coming from Marriott directly. After all, hundreds of millions of Marriott customers' email addresses were part of the breach, so do not assume any email claiming to be from Marriott or Starwood Hotels & Resorts is legitimate. That also means you should never click on any link, image, or file attached to such an email. But if you read my first book, you would already be on top of this.

I recommend that anyone who feels they might be at risk get a free copy of their credit report at www.annualcreditreport.com or call 1-877-322-8228. Everyone is entitled to one free copy per year of their credit report from any of the three major credit bureaus. Post breach, consumers should regularly and carefully check their bank statements for any suspicious activity. If anything looks even slightly out of the ordinary, contact your bank right away.

The scope and potential damage of this breach is monumental and cannot be overstated. While the largest Yahoo breach numbered around three billion users, it was more limited to personal login information, such as usernames and passwords. This Marriott breach included so many more intimate pieces of data that are sometimes hard for hackers and thieves to obtain and are potentially more damaging.

Putting the credit card numbers aside for the moment, information like dates of birth and passport numbers are a real concern. Marriott has already agreed to pay for new passports "if fraud has taken place," but as we say, the damage has already been done. Or has it? The real damage begins only after the breach has occurred and can last for years. One could easily imagine a scenario involving stolen passport numbers used to create fraudulent identities. These identities purchase many items with no intention of ever paying. According to Interpol, lost and stolen travel documents have more than doubled worldwide to over fifty million per year.[41]

THE RAMIFICATIONS

We will likely see large fines and lawsuits drag on for years as a result of the Marriott data breach. The fact

---

41   Giulia Paravacini, "EU's Passport Fraud 'Epidemic,'" Politico, January 28, 2016, https://www.politico.eu/article/europes-fake-forged-stolen-passport-epidemic-visa-free-travel-rights/.

that Starwood Division's guest reservation database was compromised by an unauthorized party opens the door to many problems, including General Data Protection Regulation (GDPR) laws for EU citizens. Under GDPR, any breaches of personal data must be reported within seventy-two hours, which was not met in this instance. Steep fines can also accrue, up to 4 percent of annual revenue for all noncompliant organizations. And then there's the reputational damage that can plague a company years after the initial sting and subsequent hefty fines. Next time you are comparison shopping on Hotels.com or Expedia for your small business, will the Marriott brand work for or against those searches?

In order to minimize the public relations nightmare of a breach and simultaneously retain existing customers, Marriott is providing guests with one year of free WebWatcher fraud consultation services. Some would refer to such services as "peace of mind" security, but for me, basic monitoring tends to function more like "peace of blind" because they generally review only a small part of users' overall security profile. WebWatcher provides users with early warning alerts if evidence of their personal data is found across the web, but services like these do not prevent anything unless users can gain insight from the alerts and act on that knowledge. When I looked into WebWatcher further, one thing that concerned me was the requirement for users to supply a wealth of personal information in order to enroll.

I don't want to completely disparage monitoring services like WebWatcher and the popular LifeLock. They provide information and help to educate their users. I use Cyberlitica, which asks only for a single email in order to scan the Dark Web. Once scanned, all associated emails, passwords, and login credentials for that email address being sold on the Dark Web are listed for the user to take action. Since this type of exposure is a clear and immediate threat to anyone's security, users have a strong motivation to take action by changing passwords, enabling multifactor authentication, and tightening their digital footprints. The following is a Cyberlitica[42] snapshot from a single email I supplied to them.

While my security habits might be a little more advanced than the typical user's, keep in mind that I have been actively promoting my small business and *Hacked Again* for the past several years. Promotion of any kind is like a pheromone for crooks looking to cash in on success at any level. So my public profile is actively inhibiting my security and privacy proportionally. Similarly, high-profile targets like Marriott make for big payoffs when hackers can ascertain and exploit their weak spots. I guess it comes with the territory.

---

42   Provided with permission from Cyberlitica.

Cyberlitica
Enterprise Threat Intelligence

Email	Breach Name	Breach Domain	Breach Date	Information Breached	Description
scott@bwsystems.com	Adapt	adapt.io	2018-11-05	Email addresses, Employers, Job titles, Names, Phone numbers, Physical addresses, Social media profiles	In November 2018, security researcher Bob Diachenko identified an unprotected database hosted by data aggregator 'Adapt'. A provider of 'Fresh Quality Contacts', the service exposed over 9.3M unique records of individuals and employer information including their names, employers, job titles, contact information and data relating to the employer including organisation description, size and revenue. No response was received from Adapt when contacted.
scott@bwsystems.com	Apollo	apollo.io	2018-07-23	Email addresses, Employers, Geographic locations, Job titles, Names, Phone numbers, Salutations, Social media profiles	In July 2018, the sales engagement startup Apollo left a database containing billions of data points publicly exposed without a password. The data was discovered by security researcher Vinny Troia who subsequently sent a subset of the data containing 126 million unique email addresses to Have I Been Pwned. The data left exposed by Apollo was used in their 'revenue acceleration platform' and included personal information such as names and email addresses as well as professional information including places of employment, the roles people hold and where they're located. Apollo stressed that the exposed data did not include sensitive information such as passwords, social security numbers or financial data. The Apollo website has a contact form for those looking to get in touch with the organisation.
scott@bwsystems.com	B2BUSABusinesses		2017-07-18	Email addresses, Employers, Job titles, Names, Phone numbers, Physical addresses	In mid-2017, a spam list of over 105 million individuals in corporate America was discovered online. Referred to as 'B2B USA Businesses', the list categorised email addresses by employer, providing information on individuals' job titles plus their work phone numbers and physical addresses. Read more about spam lists in HIBP.
scott@bwsystems.com	DataAndLeads	dataandleads.com	2018-11-14	Email addresses, Employers, IP addresses, Job titles, Names, Phone numbers, Physical addresses	In November 2018, security researcher Bob Diachenko identified an unprotected database believed to be hosted by a data aggregator. Upon further investigation, the data was linked to marketing company Data & Leads. The exposed Elasticsearch instance contained over 44M unique email addresses along with names, IP and physical addresses, phone numbers and employment information. No response was received from Data & Leads when contacted by Bob and their site subsequently went offline.
scott@bwsystems.com	Disqus	disqus.com	2012-07-01	Email addresses, Passwords, Usernames	In October 2017, the blog commenting service Disqus announced they'd suffered a data breach. The breach dated back to July 2012 but wasn't identified until years later when the data finally surfaced. The breach contained over 17.5 million unique email addresses and usernames. Users who created logins on Disqus had salted SHA1 hashes of passwords whilst users who logged in via social providers only had references to those accounts.
scott@bwsystems.com	Exactis	exactis.com	2018-06-01	Credit status information, Dates of birth, Education levels, Email addresses, Ethnicities, Family structure, Financial investments, Genders, Home ownership statuses, Income levels, IP addresses, Marital statuses, Names, Net worths, Occupations, Personal interests, Phone numbers, Physical addresses, Religions, Spoken languages	In June 2018, the marketing firm Exactis inadvertently publicly leaked 340 million records of personal data. Security researcher Vinny Troia of Night Lion Security discovered the leak contained multiple terabytes of personal information spread across hundreds of separate fields including addresses, phone numbers, family structures and extensive profiling data. The data was collected as part of Exactis' service as a 'compiler and aggregator of premium business & consumer data' which they then sell for profiling and marketing purposes. A small subset of the exposed fields were provided to Have I Been Pwned and contained 132 million unique email addresses.

POP QUIZ:
What should you do if you think your identity or accounts have been compromised?

A. Monitor your email address and accounts for fraudulent activity.

B. Respond to the warning email you have received.

C. Subscribe to a monitoring service such as Lifelock or WebWatcher.

CHAPTER 14

Opening a Can of Cyber Worms

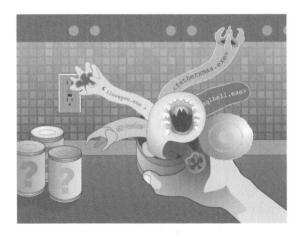

Typical ransomware attacks initially rely on users to activate and spread the malware through their own networks, but with proper cyber education, firewalls, and backups in place, ransomware is rarely a threat or even a possibility. However, the spate of WannaCry ransomware attacks, which began in 2017 and continue to this day, are uniquely disturbing because they are a new threat wrapped in the body of an old enemy. This body is not like a microscopic intruder that invades our cells to spread disease; it independently worms its way through our systems solely to harm our vital resources.

Viruses might get all the headlines these days, but computer worms are a voracious threat and enemy to all users. I would give the virus's publicist a raise and fire the worm's publicist. Just look at the fear that viruses (both medical and cyber) instill in us. Meanwhile, worms are associated with slow-moving bait and have cute nicknames like night crawler. Let's put the public images aside and deal with the reality.

ORIGINS OF COMPUTER WORMS

Computer worms were first discovered on the internet back in the late 1980s but were predated a few years by the first virus found on the internet. Both are forms of malware that spread through computer systems, but worms actually move faster and with more purpose. Viruses attach themselves to executables and use those files to transfer among systems. Worms, however, do *not* need executable files to replicate. Worms replicate and spread by themselves, disguised as system files in order to move within and beyond computer networks.

Since viruses rely on executable files, they are also relying on naïve users to activate the executables, but the same way that prophylactics and sex education help temper the spread of STDs, so do modern operating systems. A variety of user interactions, passwords, and firewalls must be overcome in modern operating systems for any user to install an executable file. This can be annoying when you need to update your browser's flash plug-in every other day, but all of those steps and checks work to keep your system uncluttered and virus free. Worms face no such impediments. They move freely and are hard to detect. Perhaps this is why worms have enjoyed a renaissance more recently thanks in part to ransomware attacks like WannaCry.

WANNACRY

Within twenty-four hours of the first wave of WannaCry ransomware attacks in May 2017, over 230,000 computers in 150 countries were reportedly infected. Britain's National Health Service, FedEx, and Spain's Telefonica were all hit hard. As a result, packages were not being shipped, people with emergencies were turned away by hospitals unable to access patient data, and telecommunications got knocked out. Collectively, these seemingly isolated attacks took the form of a global cyberwar. And with these exploits in the wild and so many older, unpatched, and vulnerable Windows PCs, it's only a matter of time before copycat hackers deploy more targeted attacks. I suppose this is part of the reason why we see the old nomenclature of "worm" being replaced by the updated "cyberworm" term.

ETERNALBLUE

The years of collecting Windows XP security holes finally caught up with the NSA. In April 2017, the elite Russian hacker group known as the Shadow Brokers publicly leaked hacking tools developed by the NSA. EternalBlue, a cyberworm developed to spread malware across networks by targeting computers, was created by the NSA to exploit a transport protocol within a Windows server vulnerability by the same name. Although the NSA has never publicly admitted it, Microsoft and numerous sources corroborate its origin and existence. EternalBlue quickly spread across networks, infecting routers, operating systems, and even SWIFT banking networks.

So who's to blame in this instance? I suppose some blame can be shared among all associated parties. It's easiest to blame the hackers who leaked the exploits to everyone, but this malware would be harmless to any modern operating system that was properly patched. Windows XP is over seventeen years old—notably not much older than the average hacker—and infamously riddled with security exploits, so I have trouble mustering compassion for the huge organizations that were affected. They could've prevented these attacks and disruptions by simply budgeting for minimum security standards long ago.

What about Microsoft? They first created this entire issue by allowing a security flaw that could be so easily exploited. To its credit, Microsoft issued a Windows XP security patch in March 2017. I give them credit since they weren't required to patch an aged operating system they no longer support. Perhaps more exploits will surface for XP and other OSs, but until then, I give Microsoft a pass on this incident.

The NSA also shares blame, not just for creating tools to spy on us but also for hoarding those tools in an unsecure manner. When EternalBlue was leaked, it was one of *five* large releases to the public, which tells me that the NSA tools were collected together during a security breach.

Breaches make for big headlines because they almost always involve huge numbers. When millions of emails or passwords are stolen all at once, it is because they were all stockpiled together somewhere in an unsecured network. NSA's obsession with spying on citizens appears to be matched only by their own security incompetence.

RANSOMWARE HACKERS

Finally, we have the ransomware hackers themselves. I see no redeeming value in an individual who holds businesses', universities', and hospitals' data for ransom. The dangers to customer accounts, reputations, and even lives cannot be overstated. On the other hand, after the first wave of ransomware settled and eventually dispersed, we were left with a lesson I have always suspected. According to Tom Bossert, assistant to the president for homeland security and counterterrorism, only $70,000 total has been extorted from many WannaCry ransomware victims, but none of those payments led to any data recovery at all.[43]

So we know that ransomware can be foiled through security education, virus-detection software, and regular data backups, but now we also know that most ransomware promises to recover data are false. Of course some data hijackers do make good on their promises, but that doesn't make doing business with them feel any better. No one wants to do business with a criminal, which is why I have repeatedly mentioned the only three things you need to do.

_____

43   Barney Jopson and Hannah Kuchler, "US Official Defends NSA over WannaCry Cyber Attack," _Financial Times_, May 15, 2017, https://www.ft.com/content/74ae2600-39a3-11e7-ac89-b01cc67cfeec.

Besides education, firewalls, and backups, the fourth rule is as simple as it is obvious: Don't pay the ransom! Hackers share all of their victims' identities with each other, so it's also like purposely adding your email to spam lists. Pay one ransom and you can expect many others trying to hack you or your small business in the future.

 POP QUIZ:
The most proactive defense against ransomware is to:

A. Purchase comprehensive cybersecurity insurance.

B. Back up your data regularly.

C. Regularly update all your devices and software with the latest security patches.

CHAPTER 15

The Internet of Stings

One of the greatest threats any online retail business can suffer is downtime. In 2018, Amazon suffered a mere sixty-three-minute outage during its annual Prime Day sales extravaganza. That hour of downtime led to an estimated $100 million loss of revenue. Small businesses won't suffer revenue losses on that scale, but they can suffer in even more devastating ways. Fortunately, the minor Distributed Denial of Service (DDoS) attack my own company's online store suffered, which was chronicled in *Hacked Again*, was brief and ultimately inconsequential, but it was my wakeup call.

DDOS MITIGATION

By design, all DDoS attacks prevent or impair information system resources or services. This can occur when a targeted website is flooded with traffic that overwhelms the server to the point where no users can access the site. Since there are so many sources of data traffic on the internet, one would think that DDoS attacks would be unstoppable, but there are precautions and remedies for such attacks. DDoS mitigation software works by identifying normal server conditions for network traffic at a given time of day and compares those to the latest traffic patterns. If any anomalies are detected, the traffic can be instantly filtered through deep packet inspection and "blacklisting" (list of data or sources that are not allowed and have been determined to be a threat), as well as "whitelisting" (list of known safe data and sources that are allowed). DDoS mitigation is effective for protecting servers from only a few bad actors at one time, so what happens when many major servers across the internet are attacked at the same time by an IoT botnet?

THE MIRAI BOTNET ATTACK

On October 21, 2016, the world witnessed one of the largest DDoS attacks in internet history. The Mirai botnet attack is not the largest,[44] but it was the most significant because it was a global attack on the popular internet services host Dyn. A botnet attack is a group of computers, smart appliances, or any internet-connected device that has been hacked and used for illicit purposes. This particular attack led to massive outages of highly trafficked websites, including the *Guardian*, Reddit, the *New York Times*, Netflix, Twitter, CNN, and many more, for most of that day. This particular DDoS attack is also significant because it was the first to leverage some six hundred thousand infected Internet of Things (IoT) devices, although only an estimated 10 to 20 percent of those devices were actively involved. All IoT devices are network-connected appliances, including cameras, routers, switches, and even your occasional smart fridge. In the case of Mirai, the botnet army primarily consisted of older devices that were easily infected due to their older, less-secure firmware and lack of secure password protections.

Most of these same devices continue to operate to this day, and that is perhaps the most worrisome problem with IoT security. The lack of security standards in modern IoT appliances is one thing, but as the devices begin to accumulate and enjoy more mainstream adoption by consumers, the Internet of Things feels more like a ticking time bomb than the future of wireless connectivity—death by a billion paper cuts. With over thirty-one billion active devices forecast to be connected by 2020, it's hard to believe we won't see another Mirai attack, only one

---

44   In 2018, GitHub experienced peak incoming data at 1.35 terabytes per second (TBps), making it the largest DDoS attack to date.

thousand times larger, and I haven't even mentioned the data-collection issues.

All IoT devices have networked sensors that collect massive amounts of data on users. Some of that data is benign, but some of it can be very personal and damaging in the wrong hands. When hackers control millions of these devices, they are also accessing millions of passwords, usernames, and metadata, including locations, video streams, and communications among unsuspecting users.

HOW IT WORKED

The Mirai botnet attack employed mostly "dumb" consumer devices consisting of security cameras, routers, and even baby monitors, but the attack against Dyn has been described as sophisticated. Like any hive community, individual drones are not particularly dangerous, but when every drone is synchronously mustered for battle, they can overwhelm the largest of opponents. I am highly allergic to and terrified of bee stings, so I call this strategy the "Internet of Stings." Many experts assumed that due to the large-scale nature and loss of productivity that resulted, the Mirai attack must have been perpetrated by a nation-state putting the United States on alert before the upcoming presidential elections—or perhaps an up-and-coming hacker group manifesting some serious skills.

In the end, the culprit turned out to be a twenty-one-year-old Rutgers University student who was just trying to get ahead in *Minecraft*. Those of you with children might recall *Minecraft* as that LEGO-like, world-building online game that occupied the better part of a day for ninety-one million players at its peak in 2018. *Minecraft* might not be as competitively cutthroat as the likes of a *Fortnite* (released mid-2017) or *World of Warcraft* (initially released at the end of 2004), but it still enjoys a growing economy fueled by players who purchase tools and skins for their characters. Low latency and minimum downtimes become highly valued attributes among *Minecraft* servers and bring in upward of $100,000 per month to the hosts. This high-demand economy led to every competitive advantage being for sale, including targeted DDoS attacks on rival servers.

Initial reports pointed to hackers with juvenile motivations behind the botnet attacks, but as the US Justice Department dug deeper into the case, the claims of simply trying to juice *Minecraft* competition began to ring false. According to authorities, former Rutgers student and self-described "untouchable hacker god" Paras Jha and two associates had already created and launched malicious computer code against the university's networks in 2014. After that, Rutgers announced a plan to spend $3 million to upgrade its computer security but was taunted by a Twitter user called "exfocus" with tweets like "where internet go?? 3m dollar gone?"[45]

A few years later, authorities contend that Jha continued to anonymously taunt Rutgers University and encouraged them to purchase DDoS protection services. At the time, Jha was president and cofounder of a DDoS mitigation company called ProTraf Solutions. Then in

---

45   Ted Sherman, "Former Rutgers U. Student Hacker Gets Home Confinement, Has to Pay $8.6M in Restitution," NJ.com, October 26, 2019, https://www.nj.com/news/2018/10/former_ru_student_hacker_ordered_to_pay_86m_in_res.html.

September 2016, massive DDoS attacks took down the popular cybersecurity website KrebsonSecurity.com for nearly four days, followed by the Mirai botnet attack that took down huge chunks of the internet. Jha plead guilty in January 2017 after investigators and bandwidth-hosting services, such as Akamai, began to notice distinct patterns that all originated with *Minecraft* code but had been spun out to target cheap IoT devices concentrated in Brazil, Colombia, Vietnam, and China. Dozens of iterations on the already-released open source code and an additional pair of hacker friends from Pennsylvania and New Orleans led authorities to a new conclusion: the *Minecraft* DDoS attacks were merely a proof of concept for these industrious hackers. For his crimes, Jha received a hefty $8.6 million restitution judgment as well as five year's probation, twenty-five hundred hours of community service, and additional fines for him and his two codefendants.

These hackers' ultimate goal appeared to be the sale of large-scale DDoS attacks aimed at *specific* websites or networks. Sure enough, days after reporting on large-scale DDoS activity across the internet, security researcher Brian Krebs became a victim himself when his own website was targeted. The attack was so intense that it not only knocked out his website, it also forced Akamai, a leading content delivery network (CDN) to drop Krebs from its hosting network due to the sustained DDoS attacks it was experiencing. With traditional DDoS attacks, companies can employ a filter for incoming web traffic or simply increase the bandwidth; however, in this unprecedented attack, all traditional DDoS mitigation techniques failed due to the sheer volume. DDoS attacks are fairly common across the web, so how did this attack get so large and out of hand?

Forensic security team Imperva Incapsula discovered some interesting details, including a high degree of territoriality. Specifically, Mirai included malware with several scripts designed to eradicate other worms and Trojans, as well as prohibit remote connection attempts by any hijacked IoT devices. Like a competitive online game, this malware was created to completely pwn the opposition. In the gaming world, "pwn" means to completely obliterate and own an opponent: in this case, that meant everyone, including IoT device owners, fellow hackers, and a large chunk of the internet. Another note of interest is the open source nature of Mirai. Open source code is generally preferred among security experts, users, and most companies too. It allows many programmers to publicly debug and troubleshoot coding issues without signing an NDA or working for a large data company. It's a community effort, but I suppose all community efforts can be co-opted to serve bad actors.

PRECAUTIONS

If you are concerned about the security of your IoT devices at home or in your business, there are some basic precautions that can be easily taken to avoid becoming the unwilling victim of DDoS attacks. Make sure all of your devices—routers, network printers, computers, networked cameras, networked smart-home appliances, etc.—are set up with unique usernames and passwords. Perform a quick Google search on a model number or manufacturer to determine their history of updates. If you see a pattern of complaints from users regarding a lack of updating or support for any device, consider replacing it, if possible, with something better supported.

Avoid purchasing and using any cheap devices unless no competitor offers the same performance and features. You can also visit various security-focused websites that perform quick and free scans of all devices on your network to make sure you are not vulnerable to some of the more aggressive DDoS attacks out there.

With so many attack vectors and no unifying security standard, IoT devices are poised to become a big part of the cybersecurity narrative over the next few years. Be sure to stay on the right side of this battle by not purchasing IoT technology needlessly; make sure it is vital to your business and has been vetted as secure. No one can guarantee safety from DDoS attacks, but if we all do our part to minimize the number of weakly secured devices, we can ensure that the Internet of Things will not become the Internet of Stings.

 POP QUIZ:
What's the best way to steer clear of IoT device security hacks?

A. Choose only name-brand hardware makers.

B. Disconnect IoT devices from the internet when you are not using them.

C. Do not use or connect any IoT devices you do not need.

CHAPTER 16

Equifax and What Not to Do When You Are Hacked

Imagine that you start a new business with a silent partner you've never met. This silent partner acts like an accountant. You never really asked for them, but they came with the business in order to go through your finances to help you get loans for future expansion—all for free. Sounds like a pretty sweet deal, right? Here's the rub: even though you never consented or even met this partner, they have access to all of your personal information, such as Social Security number, bank and credit statements, driver's license, filed tax forms, etc. Then you come to find out that they have been careless with your private information, leaving it out in the open across the internet. You try to stop it, but it's too late. Your personal and financial data have been exposed for at least six weeks. The silent partner knew about it but didn't tell you. You try to fire them, but you can't—they come with the business, and you never really hired them in the first place. In an attempt to make amends, this inept partner offers you a year of service for free, the same service you never asked for and never paid for to begin with.

This nightmare scenario is a very real thing because it already happened to at least 146 million people in 2017, courtesy of the Equifax hack.

CREDIT REPORTING AGENCIES

There are four consumer credit reporting agencies: TransUnion, Experian, Equifax, and Innovis.[46] Of the four, Equifax is the oldest. Founded in 1899, Equifax is headquartered in Atlanta with annual revenues in excess of $3 billion. Equifax is a publicly traded company on the New York Stock Exchange (symbol EFX) and has over nine thousand employees spread on fourteen countries. Credit reporting agencies are required by US law to provide consumers with one free credit report every year. Equifax also sells

---

46   Innovis is not included in the larger ones known as the Big Three.

fraud prevention services directly to consumers and offers credit monitoring, which I find rather ironic, considering the massive breach they have suffered. It's a little like an Alcoholics Anonymous counselor inviting members to happy hour at the bar down the street where he's a bartender.

Equifax aggregates information from over eight hundred million individual consumers, as well as from eighty-eight million businesses around the globe. Needless to say, Equifax has an enormous amount of PI, meaning "personal information," on people, including 75 percent of all Americans. Any company with that much PI should do anything and everything to protect that information. After all, that data is not just for marketing purposes, although Equifax treats it as such; that data is their lifeblood and the only reason for their existence and revenues. You could say that such a large, important, and valuable data set—as well as Equifax's ability to protect it—is their core competency. So what happened?

THE BREACH DAMAGE

Equifax became the victim of a massive cybersecurity breach that began sometime in mid-May but was not discovered until July 29, 2017, according to ex-Equifax CEO Rick Smith and confirmed by Equifax. The details went public when they announced it on September 7, 2017, alerting the world that cybercriminals stole close to 146 million US Equifax consumers' personal data. Over two hundred thousand consumer credit card credentials were also stolen in the attack. In addition, approximately eight thousand Canadians and somewhere between four hundred thousand and forty-four million UK residents have been affected by the Equifax breach.[47]

As with most breaches, people's names, addresses, and birth dates were compromised. But since this breach involved one of the Big Three credit agencies, drivers' license numbers, credit card numbers, and three-quarters of all US Social Security numbers were also exposed. The amount of data taken from this breach alone is staggering, but when added to an array of others—including institutional government breaches like Office of Personnel Management or OPM (March 2014), payment processor breaches like Heartland Payment Systems' (March 2008), retail breaches like Target's (December 2013), financial institutions breaches like J. P. Morgan's (July 2014), social network breaches like AdultFriendFinder's (October 2016), and internet service provider breaches like Yahoo's (September 2016)—a disturbing reality begins to emerge. More on that in a bit, but I don't want to lump Equifax in with all the other breaches because it has earned a special place in the "Scammers That Got Scammed" hall of shame.

On September 15, 2017, Equifax shared an official statement detailing the hiring of Mandiant on August 2, 2017, to begin an internal investigation. Mandiant is a prominent American cybersecurity firm that provides incident response services and became well known in 2013 when it released a report that directly implicated China in cyber espionage.

---

47   John Leyden, "44m UK Consumers on Equifax's Books. How Many Pwned? Blighty Eagerly Awaits Spex on the Breach," *The Register*, September 11, 2017, https://www. theregister.co.uk/2017/09/11/equifax_breach_uk_exposure/.

Equifax reported the breach was a result of a flaw in Apache Struts, an open-source web application framework used in developing Java web applications. It is important to note that a patch for the known vulnerability was released on March 7, 2017, two months before the attack occurred. However, Equifax did not apply the security patch update until after it was already too late.

SLOPPY SECURITY

Security patches for software applications and operating systems are regularly released when new vulnerabilities surface, but the onus is always on the user or company's IT team to update swiftly. All too often, companies get complacent and put off what should be immediately addressed. But this was not the single point of failure for Equifax, as there were additional contributing factors, such as a poor and insecure network design that did not implement proper segmentations. Individual databases should always be segmented from one another; otherwise, hackers can easily gain access to all data through a breach at a single point of entry.

There have also been reports of inadequate encryption of identifiable personal information. The topper was a series of ineffective breach-detection mechanisms that were in place, which might explain Equifax's molasses-like reaction and subsequent late announcement of the breach. However, we've seen evidence to suggest that the Equifax top brass actually concealed these facts and postponed public announcements in order to avoid penalties and cash out of the company before the bottom fell out.

On September 15, 2017, Equifax released a statement regarding the immediate departure and subsequent replacement of their chief information officer (CIO) and chief security officer (CSO). Three days after Equifax disclosed the July 2017 breach, Congressman Barry Loudermilk (R-GA), who was coincidently given thousands of dollars from Atlanta-based Equifax, introduced a bill to *reduce* consumer protections for the nation's credit bureaus. The bill also included a cap for potential damages in any class action suit up to $500,000 regardless of the amount of loss or class size. Furthermore, the bill eliminated all possible punitive damages.[48] This proposal upset many consumer groups, including the National Association of Consumer Advocates (NACA) and Georgia Watch.

"Equifax's use of forced arbitration clauses and class action bans means that consumers cannot band together in court to seek remedies against it," said Liz Coyle, executive director of Georgia Watch. "This is unacceptable and will have disastrous effects on the marketplace."[49]

Congressman Loudermilk has since withdrawn his bill due to mounting pressure from consumer groups, like NACA, and the Democrats' threats of counter bills that would further punish companies like Equifax for harming Americans.

---

48   NACA, "Georgia Congressman Must Withdraw His EQUIFAX-Friendly Bill," National Association of Consumer Advocates, September 8, 2017, https://www.consumeradvocates.org/media/press-release/georgia-congressman-must-withdraw-his-equifax-friendly-bill.

49   NACA, "Georgia Congressman Must Withdraw His EQUIFAX-Friendly Bill," National Association of Consumer Advocates, September 8, 2017, https://www.consumeradvocates.org/media/press-release/georgia-congressman-must-withdraw-his-equifax-friendly-bill.

EQUIFAX'S MODE OF "DAMAGE CONTROL"

Just before Equifax publicly acknowledged its breach, there was a small but suspicious change made to the customer terms of services agreement on the company website. The amended agreement now included an arbitration clause with a class action waiver. Visible by merely logging into the Equifax website to verify whether their information was compromised, all Equifax customers learned they would automatically be bound to arbitration in the event of future lawsuits. This meant that no customer could bring a case to public trial for a jury of their peers to decide. Nor could the victims join together in a class action lawsuit to collect damages. Consumer watchdog groups and customers were not happy.

Forced-arbitration clauses are not uncommon when the company offering services is itself compromised. In the case of the massive Target retail store breach back in 2014, Experian offered one free year of credit-monitoring services to all consumers affected. But since Experian itself hadn't been breached at that time, consumers were allowed to join together and file class action lawsuits against Target for damages incurred from that breach.

However, in this instance, Equifax was a victim of the attack, so its corporate interests were put before its own customers to ensure that damages long after the hack would be minimized. After so many blunders were revealed, it was clear that Equifax's true allegiance was to itself and the shareholders. On a capsizing ship full of passengers, Equifax is the shameless captain quietly stepping onto the heads of those drowning in order to get into the lifeboat first. The company has since issued a statement clarifying the confusion and suspicion and has removed the arbitration clause from its website.

"FIXES" THAT FIXED NOTHING

But the Equifax website woes didn't stop there. I would be derelict in my cybersecurity duty if I didn't emphasize just how poorly this entire data breach was handled. On October 8, 2017, security researcher Brian Krebs reported that The Work Number, a website under Equifax's TALX division, had exposed salary histories for tens of thousands of employees in US companies simply by entering in their Social Security numbers.[50] Since more than half the US population's Social Security numbers have compromised by the Equifax breach, it's easy for hackers, blackmailers, and conmen to access all the associated confidential information. These salary details could effectively be used to target high-net-worth individuals with ransomware attacks or IRS fraud. A few days later, it was also reported that the Equifax website was sending visitors to a link with a fake update for Adobe Flash.

By now, you should be all too familiar with the weak security of Adobe's Flash platform. As far as I'm concerned, it should be avoided at all costs. After all, Flash is a dying platform that Adobe itself has vowed to no longer support after 2020. In the meantime, hackers routinely exploit security holes either by infusing unsecured web-based

---

50   Krebs on Security, "Equifax Breach Fallout: Your Salary History," October 8, 2017, https://krebsonsecurity.com/2017/10/equifax-breach-fallout-your-salary-history/.

Flash content—in the form of ads, games, or pop-ups—with malware or by tricking individuals into updating to the latest "secure" version of Flash, which is simply a Trojan virus, meaning malware that's disguised as legitimate software waiting to be deployed into the system.

In a further irony, Equifax set up a website for consumers concerned about the breach. This new website was supposedly created to provide customers with details on the security status of their information by entering their last name and the last six digits of their Social Security numbers. Security researchers revealed the website ran stock WordPress with a flawed TLS implementation. And the domain name wasn't even registered to Equifax, so you didn't have to be a security expert to realize that this looked a lot like a phishing website set up to collect Social Security numbers. Researchers quickly realized that by making up any last name and typing in any random digits, the website would tell that fictitious person whether their data may have been exposed from the breach. Other researchers received different security warnings, even after entering the exact same information. It appeared to be a random security-warning generator. But one detail wasn't random: after each entry, users would be prompted to enroll into Equifax's TrustID paid-protection services.

HOW TO PROTECT YOURSELF
Anytime a website asks for any portion of a Social Security number, immediately stop what you are doing and reevaluate. Look at the email or link that might have prompted you to visit this website and the URL of the page

you are on. Determine the website you want to visit and manually type it into your browser. If the link is too long to type, take the time to navigate through the website to reach your final URL destination. Even partial Social Security numbers are gold to hackers and can cause a feeding frenzy on the Dark Web.

One thing that Equifax has demonstrated is that it cannot be trusted with our private information, so for as much as I was curious about the status of my own information, I never even considered checking in with Equifax. Instead, I simply double-checked all of my credit and banking statements for unusual activity, which is something we should all be doing on a regular basis anyway.

FOLLOW THE MONEY

Another highly suspicious chapter in this story concerns three Equifax executives selling off $1.8 million of their Equifax shares just days after the beach was discovered, which also happened to be more than full month *before* the breach was publicly announced.[51] Even if you give the executives the benefit of the doubt and assume they somehow didn't connect their actions with the breach, they still allegedly broke the law. This would be a clear violation of Security and Exchange Commission (SEC) laws, not to mention of the public trust and fellow Equifax shareholders. On September 18, Bloomberg

---

51   Alina Selyukh, "3 Equifax Executives Sold Stock Days After Hack That Wasn't Disclosed For A Month," NPR, September 8, 2017, https://www.npr.org/sections/thetwo-way/2017/09/08/549434187/3-equifax-executives-sold-stock-days-after-hack-that-wasnt-disclosed-for-a-month.

revealed that the US Department of Justice (DOJ) had opened an investigation to determine whether the three executives had violated any insider trading laws.[52]

Since then, an internal committee formed by Equifax determined that the three executives had no knowledge of the breach, but the DOJ and SEC investigations continue. This is partly due to the need for a truly impartial investigation but also due to further incriminating patterns. In March 2018, former Equifax executive Jun Ying was charged with insider trading as a result of selling nearly $1 million worth of the company's shares before Equifax's massive data breach was made public.[53] Jun Ying was reported to be the company's next global CIO but had allegedly used confidential information entrusted to him by the company that Equifax had suffered a significant breach, which hadn't yet been disclosed. The fact that Mr. Ying exercised all of his vested Equifax stock options, followed by selling the shares and benefiting from close to $1 million in proceeds, is troubling.

In March 2017, just a few months before the major breach, it was revealed that Equifax had suffered another breach earlier in the year. The earlier breach wasn't nearly as large in scale and potential damage, but it appeared to prompt another large stock sell-off by Equifax CFO John Gamble, the very same CFO who also sold off nearly $1

52   Tom Schoenberg, Anders Melin, and Matt Robinson, "Equifax Stock Sales Are the Focus of U.S. Criminal Probe," Bloomberg, September 18, 2017, https://www.bloomberg.com/news/articles/2017-09-18/equifax-stock-sales-said-to-be-focus-of-u-s-criminal-probe.

53   Stacy Cowley, "Ex-Equifax Executive Charged With Insider Trading Tied to '17 Breach," *New York Times*, March 14, 2018, https://www.nytimes.com/2018/03/14/business/equifax-executive-insider-trading.html.

million in holdings along with his fellow executives later. I have no doubt this incriminating tidbit of information will be revisited in the final DOJ report. Again, if we assume this CFO was in the dark on both breaches and had only good intentions with no inclination toward insider trading, then why weren't he and the other executives named in the investigation notified by Equifax staff or an internal memo about the possibility of a breach? Are cybersecurity matters this grave *really* only reserved for the CEO and a few geeks in IT? Doubtful. Equifax has three primary jobs: collect, evaluate, and protect all of our data. Regardless of what we think about its performance of the first two jobs, the company failed, hands down, at protecting our data.

On February 27, 2019, it was Equifax CEO Mark Begor's turn to be grilled. During a congressional hearing, he was asked by Congresswoman Katie Porter (D-CA) whether he would consider sharing *his* address, birth date, and Social Security number publicly. Begor uncomfortably responded that he would rather not. The congresswoman went on to question why the Equifax attorneys were seeking to dismiss a class action suit over the 2017 breach. They argued that no harm had occurred and yet feared the harm that could occur from revealing their own personal data. After that, rising star Congresswoman Alexandria Ocasio-Cortez (D-NY) laid into him about collecting all of our consumer data without consent. CEO Begor justified his actions by describing the tools consumers can use to lock or freeze their credit data. Ocasio-Cortez noted that one in five US consumers has at least one error in their credit reports. She went on to compare that ratio to a skydiver's parachute. "I don't think a lot of people would be skydiving," Ocasio-Cortez finished.

The fact that top executives are making decisions and selling shares in their company while "flying blind" on cybersecurity matters is unacceptable. If ever there were a "need-to-know" position on a "need-to-know" matter, it would be the CFO of Equifax. The chief financial officer's first responsibility is managing the financial risks of the company and then reporting directly to the CEO with that information. So how could the Equifax CFO effectively manage any risks if they are not immediately informed of their own company's security integrity at any given moment?

It's clear that Equifax's unconscionable actions resulted from a toxic cocktail of hubris, ignorance, greed, deception, and a wee bit of bad luck. What isn't so clear is just how much we have all been affected by their incompetence. I began this chapter with an imaginary partner allusion to Equifax. We might need its services at specific times in our lives, but that does little to temper resentment in taking on this type of silent partner. When we take a stroll down breach memory lane, we are reminded of so many violations. A partial Social Security number here, a drivers' license number there, an email, and phone number too; all of these pieces of data are parts that make up a much larger puzzle, and there is one complete puzzle for each and every adult.

The Equifax data breach was a tremendous boon to hackers everywhere. It offered essential pieces of data on tens of millions of Americans that until now were not available anywhere else. Just like a group of puzzle solvers works faster than any single person, by working together, hackers can share, trade, and sell many pieces with each other. They can combine efforts and complete puzzles for every single person in the country and eventually the world. As I see it, it's only a matter of time before we see national identity theft. It might appear that I'm trying to scare readers into action, and if this chapter truly leads to at least one person securing their digital identity, I'll cop to that scare tactic. But my true goal is to remind people that they should already be taking the security measures outlined throughout this book. Until we can agree on a new form of digital identity for everyone, shore up our weakest security tropes, and make those who fail to comply pay for their transgressions, we will never truly reset the zero-day countdown clock.

 POP QUIZ:
What will freezing your credit not affect?

A. Your vulnerability to identity theft.

B. Your credit score.

C. Your need to monitor financial statements for fraud.

CHAPTER 17

Uber's Bumpy Ride

Few startups have garnered more vitriol and praise at the same time than Uber. It began as a simple alternative to established taxi services, but quickly pivoted to the future of, well . . . everything. Investors continue to heap billions into the startup in an effort to raise its impending initial public offering (IPO) valuation and to mask a multitude of internal, social, and legal battles that still plague the company. As of this writing, both Uber and Lyft have gone public on the NYSE and NASDAQ, respectively, with both suffering significant drops in stock price below their initial public offerings.

If you've followed Uber's blunders in the news like I have, you've no doubt lost count of all of them by now, so the following is a few of their greatest hits:

- Unauthorized user tracking
- Sexual harassment at the highest corporate level
- Illegal operation in multiple countries
- Failure to report sexual assaults on passengers
- Illegally obtaining private medical records of a rape victim
- Underpaying and deceiving their drivers in a pyramid scheme–like payout
- Hiding (via Operation Greyball) service from government regulators
- Failure to obtain permits for self-driving vehicles already on the road
- Booking thousands of fake rides from competitor Lyft to disrupt their service
- Technology theft lawsuit from Waymo, owned by Google's parent company, Alphabet

And these are just the top ten headlines that can be found in seconds. These and many other missteps have led Uber CEO Travis Kalanick to step down from his own company. It's no wonder #DeleteUber continues to go viral in waves when each negative story surfaces. So with all this controversy and poor press, why has Uber continued to gain momentum and support from investors and riders?

Most of the investor support stems from the potential that ridesharing services like Uber offer. It's not so much the convenience or price or even the job creation. In fact, it's all about the job obsoletion, but more on that in a bit. In 2017, Uber burned through $2 billion of investor cash because investors are actually paying for 59 percent of all riders' fares.[54] These subsidies create Uber's incredible burn rate but also ensure that its mindshare and market share remain on top. Competing ridesharing services, such as Lyft, operate more efficiently because they have much less investor capital to throw around. In the world of tech startups, however, it's all about getting the most market share quickly. Sure, Uber has doubled bookings since 2016, but it has never made a profit and does not plan to anytime soon. Yet bullish investors keep throwing money at this high-tech "cash-burning machine," as one Bloomberg analyst put it. So if that's Uber's long game, what's the strategy?

THE UBER STRATEGY

Uber's only hope of surviving beyond 2020 is a fleet of self-driving cars. Scheduled to go public at the time of this writing, Uber is still behaving like a startup, burning through investors' cash faster than a dragster. Since it cannot afford to pay all of the human drivers for much longer and also cannot afford to lose market penetration and customers to the likes of Lyft and traditional cabs,

---

54   Kevin Kelleher, "Uber Is Still Burning Cash at a rate of $2 Billion a Year," Venture Beat, August 23, 2017, https://venturebeat.com/2017/08/23/uber-is-still-burning-cash-at-a-rate-of-2-billion-a-year/.

Uber must get as many self-driving cars on the road as quickly as possible. This is supposed to keep fares low and get every rider to their destination quickly. But what are the downsides?

Some high-tech jobs will be created with the new strategy, but most driving jobs will still be lost in all future ride-sharing economies. That is the nature of the artificial intelligence beast. AI is nothing new in job displacement; automation has been killing off factory jobs for decades, so what else has got people worried about autonomous cars? Google has been testing self-driving cards for years, and now Apple and even Amazon are also rumored to be getting into the mix.

Some carmakers like Tesla are already selling their latest electric vehicles (Model 3) fully equipped with preinstalled autonomous-driving hardware, and most other more traditional automakers have reportedly fast-tracked their own self-driving projects. Putting the necessary legislation and hazardous aberrant weather and road conditions aside for a moment, the technology challenges behind self-driving cars have been licked . . . or so we thought.

ISSUES WITH SELF-DRIVING CARS

Google's autonomous car division, Waymo, has logged over four million miles on public roads with minimal self-reported traffic incidents, but not all autonomy is created equal. In October 2018, a motorcyclist was injured in a collision with a Waymo self-driving car. Waymo claimed the incident was caused by the human driver and not the autonomous vehicle itself. That same month, Waymo won approval from the California DMV to test cars without human drivers on public roads.

Unfortunately, minor fender benders aren't the only result of autonomous car testing on public roads. In early 2018, a self-driving Volvo XC90 sport-utility vehicle owned by Uber killed a pedestrian in Tempe, Arizona. A human "safety operator" at the wheel was reportedly distracted at the time of the incident in which Elaine Herzberg, a forty-nine-year-old woman walking across the road with a bike, was struck.[55] This woman has the unfortunate distinction of being the first person ever to be killed by an autonomous vehicle. She will not be the last.

The autonomous car's interior and exterior camera video was released publicly. When I watched it, the first thing that struck me was how fast the accident occurred. I understand most accidents unfold this way and why they can't always be prevented, but there was no visual indication that the car's sensors or its braking system even detected and reacted until long after the collision. Of course, the human behind the wheel was completely caught off guard, and since then the victim's family has reached a settlement with Uber for damages. To complicate matters, the incident occurred at night at a median that included a brick pathway. This pathway—presumably encouraging pedestrians to jaywalk—is currently the

---

55   Helen Popkin, "Operator in Uber Self-Driving Crash Is a Felon. That's Not Why Elaine Herzberg Is Dead," *Forbes*, March 23, 2018, https://www.forbes.com/sites/helenpopkin/2018/03/23/operator-in-arizona-uber-self-driving-car-crash-is-a-felon-thats-not-why-elaine-herzberg-is-dead/#61524487669b.

focus of a $10 million lawsuit filed by the victim's family against the city of Tempe, but it also highlights an important issue with all autonomous vehicles.

Like any student driver, autonomous vehicles still have a lot of machine learning (meaning AI) to do. These vehicles have lightning-fast reflexes when they work correctly but not nearly enough experience to know when to proceed more slowly in certain populated areas or to avoid vehicles that appear to be driving recklessly. Perhaps one day, artificial intelligence will surpass a seasoned driver's instincts, but until then, the data gathered and implemented from tragic accidents will be a necessary evil. Like its human creator, AI improves most effectively by learning from mistakes.

Light Detection and Ranging (LIDAR) sensors are as important to autonomous vehicles as eyeballs are to human drivers. These visual "sponges" continuously suck up data for the car's brain in 360 degrees while the car's AI determines the safest course of action to the tune of trillions of operations per second. These incredible computationally intensive tasks don't come cheap, so driverless carmakers like Waymo are investing in LIDAR and AI that can cut hardware costs down by as much as 90 percent.[56] These advances are key to making self-driving cars scalable and allowing fleets to grow into the millions, thereby serving anyone at anytime with a driverless ride to anywhere. That's billions of customers served, but what about those millions of Uber drivers?

---

56   Ron Amadeo, "Google's Waymo Invests in LIDAR Technology, Cuts Costs by 90 Percent," Ars Technica, January 9, 2017, https://arstechnica.com/cars/2017/01/googles-waymo-invests-in-lidar-technology-cuts-costs-by-90-percent/.

Uber's distinct advantage is its head start in the ride-sharing business. As tarnished as it may be, it has the brand recognition to deploy millions of "autonomous cabs" around the world quicker than any other company because it's already the clear leader in ride-sharing services in North America and many other countries. But Uber can afford to reach this critical mass only by replacing all of its human drivers with unmanned fleets of vehicles. That's the downside of AI in most job sectors. Looking at any low-skill manual labor, it's clear that most of those jobs will cease to exist in about ten years, no matter how many elections are won on the promise of bringing those jobs back. But it's not all doom and gloom. Advances in AI will trickle down to every sector and improve the lives of all humans in ways we cannot yet measure.

UBER'S DATA BREACH

By now you might be wondering how all of this relates to hacking and cybersecurity. It would seem that I have buried the headline because of the many egregious actions detailed by the press over the past few years, but Uber has one more skeleton in its ride-sharing closet: in late 2016, Uber suffered a massive data breach. The personal information of fifty-seven million Uber users was accessed by hackers, including phone numbers, email addresses, and names. The hackers also stole six hundred thousand driver's licenses from Uber drivers. The data was all stored on an Amazon server in a GitHub account and accessed through a third-party cloud-based service by hackers. So far, the details of the breach are fairly pedestrian. It's how

Uber handled the entire incident from there on that raises more than a few eyebrows, followed by pitchforks.

To its credit, Uber tracked down the hackers in an effort to retrieve the data. But if you know anything about bits and bytes, you know data has no physical constraints and can exist in an infinite amount of places. So while Uber would like to present itself as a victim fighting back, it is simply paying hush money to the hackers. There was never a chance these cyber criminals would hand the breached data back to Uber because millions of copies could be made in one keystroke. Nevertheless, in exchange for $100,000, Uber made the thieves "return" the data and sign a nondisclosure agreement (NDA). In an effort to further disguise the entire incident, Uber CSO, Joe Sullivan, earmarked the $100,000 payout as a "bug bounty."[57] Uber does have a legitimate bug bounty program for security researchers that was launched back in 2015, but this payout was not part of that program. The $100,000 payout is an insult to legitimate security researchers, Uber customers, and Uber investors. It undermines every legitimate effort to stamp out bugs and security holes by creating a black market for ransoms to be demanded and paid. Simply put, it is going into business with criminals by paying them to hide this relationship.

These horrific details were first revealed on November 22, a full year after the breach was discovered by Uber's

---

57   Summer Meza, "Uber Paid 20-Year-Old Hacker Who Lives with His Mom to Cover Up Massive Data Breach," *Newsweek*, December 7, 2017, https://www.newsweek.com/uber-hack-data-breach-paid-florida-hacker-cover-740849.

security staff.[58] This was the same security staff under Travis Kalanick, Uber's CEO at the time. Since this breach has been revealed, current Uber CEO, Dara Khosrowshahi, has vowed to do better and "earn the trust of our customers,"[59] but Uber faces much more than the wrath of customers. It's safe to assume that all of the stolen data will turn up on the Dark Web in due time, meaning that millions of Uber customers will be exposed to identity theft through targeted phishing attacks. In particular, those six hundred thousand driver's licenses will go a long way to validate residency for undocumented immigrants, fetching up to one hundred dollars each on the black market. That is substantially more valuable than any email or even a stolen credit card.

THE FATE OF UBER

The repercussions of Uber's dirty little secret will live on long beyond the stolen data's lifespan value. Even if we believe Uber had the best intentions of keeping the hacked user data from being released into the wild, it broke state and possibly federal laws, as well as customer faith. Speaking of customers, Uber will certainly face civil lawsuits as soon as customers with stories of identity theft and incurred damages begin to surface. Uber will probably never see true justice, but hopefully it will eventually receive much more than a slap on

58   Julia Carrie Wong, "Uber Concealed Massive Hack That Exposed Data of 57m Users and Drivers," *Guardian*, November 22, 2017, https://www.theguardian.com/technology/2017/nov/21/uber-data-hack-cyber-attack.

59   Cory Bennett, "Uber Reveals Yearlong Cover-Up of Major Data Breach," Politico, November 21, 2017, https://www.politico.com/story/2017/11/21/uber-coverup-data-breach-186597.

the wrist. Uber's investors have deep pockets, and they also have deep roots in the tech community. Dozens of Fortune 500 companies, as well as Chinese giants like Baidu and Didi Chuxing,[60] have vested interests in Uber's success, while Uber has its own selfish interests in mind.

Uber cannot possibly last long enough to fulfill its grand scheme of millions of autonomous cars at the rate the company burns through its cash. So what will happen? Since the US federal government will ultimately have the final say on when driverless cars can populate American roadways, Uber needs to lengthen its cash runway. It has been speculated that Uber will burn through all of its cash sometime in 2019, the same year they went public.[61] The company's current valuation would see a huge bump if the IPO and publicly traded stock experience strong growth. A strong market performance would fuel Uber for several more years, which is enough time for Uber to lower operational costs and for the federal and state governments to declare the roads officially open for driverless cars. Of course, Uber faces further scrutiny in the form of the SEC and millions of shareholders, but it's used to playing the shell game with other people's money. Ultimately, the serious lack of judgment and poor security practices reveal Uber as a company that cares much more about its valuation than its users' private data.

---

60   Didi Chuxing purchased Uber's Chinese operations in exchange for a 17.7 percent stake in Uber.

61   Eric Newcomer, "Uber Revenue Growth Slows, Losses Persist as 2019 IPO Draws Near," *Economic Times*, February 16, 2019, https://economictimes.indiatimes.com/small-biz/startups/newsbuzz/uber-revenue-growth-slows-losses-persist-as-2019-ipo-draws-near/articleshow/68019800.cms.

RIDESHARING CHOICES

With both Lyft and Uber now being traded publicly, some of the tech newness and uncertainty is wearing off. This new crop of ridesharing companies are no longer the darlings of Silicon Valley they once were. They are now just two more companies that must prove themselves to investors while vying for market share and customer loyalty. As the underdog in both market share and mindshare, Lyft must grow without taking as many shortcuts as Uber did, but in order to compete with Uber, Lyft must leverage every advantage it can muster. I hope that means things like customer privacy and security won't receive short shrift in the growth process, but in the world of ridesharing startups, no news is good news—so far.

 POP QUIZ:
Which ridesharing service collects the least amount of your data?

A. Uber.

B. Lyft.

C. Public taxi service.

CHAPTER 18

Anthem's Unhealthy Breach

![puzzle piece] If you are like me, health insurance may not top your list of conversation starters, but in my business, prevention is the cornerstone of cybersecurity best practices. Perhaps this is why I waited until now to cover this topic and particular breach. Health-care costs continue to rise to hideous levels while the coverage is watered down. As a small business owner and employee with family coverage, I continue to see double-digit coverage cost increases every year in my

state of New Jersey. So what happens when the primary health insurance provider for millions of people takes one security slipup and parlays it into the single largest class action data breach settlement in history?

Anthem is a publicly traded health insurance provider with revenue reaching $90 billion per year. So how does a single cybersecurity slipup result in such a large breach? First let's back up and clarify something. According to an independent internal investigation by Mandiant,[62] a breach disaster recovery service, a subsidiary of Anthem was breached on February 18, 2014, when an employee clicked on an email attachment containing phishing malware. The malware allowed hackers to obtain remote access to that computer and approximately ninety other systems within Anthem. In early February 2015, Anthem formally announced it had suffered a massive data breach that compromised 78.8 million customer records along with 12 million records of minors. The exposed data included addresses, names, birth dates, Social Security numbers, and email addresses. So did this single act of carelessness by an employee truly result in the Anthem breach? Technically, it did—but not exactly.

As I've tried to convey throughout this book, cybersecurity is everybody's business, whether we're talking about a small business or large one like Anthem. So it is impossible to blame a single employee, computer, or weak password when there are so many other factors in play. We will probably never learn all of the details or the

---

62   Acquired by FireEye in December 2013.

extent to which Anthem was prepared for such a breach. Those details remain under cover of the full investigation, but it's easy to imagine the series of events that led up to this employee's lapse in security judgment.

Perhaps the manager or department didn't properly train employees on email security procedures or that manager wasn't properly trained. The buck can be passed all the way back to the top. If the CSO doesn't receive the proper budgeting and support from the CEO or board of directors, how can every employee down the line be expected to know the most secure protocols to follow? Show me a single cybersecurity breach, and I will show you a dozen reasons why that breach occurred.

After the dust of the breach, investigation, and legal settlement had settled, Anthem was required to provide a minimum of two years of credit monitoring to victims, as well as identity theft protection at no charge. Victims that already had credit monitoring services in place would receive full compensation plus any out-of-pocket reimbursements that were traceable to the data breach. The settlement also required Anthem to improve its information security practices, including a specific requirement for encryption of sensitive information going forward. Better late than never . . .

Some three and a half years after the breach was announced, a final judgment of $115 million was awarded to the millions of victims. Over one hundred individual lawsuits against Anthem across the country were consolidated into a single lump sum that would end further claims against Anthem over the 2015 data breach.

In addition, Anthem agreed to pay the federal government $16 million and draft a comprehensive risk analysis plan to determine its vulnerabilities and fix all security deficiencies. Anthem also agreed to spend $260 million on security-related measures going forward.[63] While these efforts are always encouraging, the sad truth is that this and many other massive compromises could have been minimized or completely avoided if those security measures had been taken in the first place.

UNTOLD AFTERMATH

Anthem spent roughly $2.5 million to engage consultants on top of the government fines and class action settlement. Its monetary losses have been contained and remediated, so the company is already back on track for a profitable quarter and year as of this writing. The customers affected by the Anthem breach received a nominal settlement, but the other shoe has not yet dropped. Millions of their Social Security numbers, names, and emails continue to be stockpiled, traded, bought, and sold. This type of data follows these customers around for years if not the rest of their lives. To make matters worse, each piece of data can be analyzed and connected to other pieces of data floating around the Dark Web. Eventually, many of these seemingly disparate data chunks will coalesce to form complete identity profiles, making a complete identity theft easy for cyberthieves and a costly nightmare for their victims.

63   Charlie Osborne, "Anthem Agrees to Pay $16 Million in Data Breach Privacy Settlement," ZDNet, October 16, 2018, https://www.zdnet.com/article/anthem-agrees-to-pay-us-gov-16-million-in-data-breach-settlement/.

In a 2017 report created by Cybersecurity Ventures, Inc., famed investor and cybersecurity entrepreneur Robert Herjavec, CEO of the Herjavec Group, said, "In 2017 we have seen more focus on cybersecurity investment from health-care providers." He continues, "They've felt the pain of their antiquated systems and have had to step up out of necessity to do more to protect their infrastructures and patient data."[64] In my experience and research into health-care breaches, Robert is correct. Health-care organizations, whether hospitals or the insurance providers that pay for expensive hospital care, are at the nexus of unsecured networks and gobs of customer and patient data.

HEALTH-CARE INSTITUTIONS ARE TARGETS

As I continue to travel for speaking engagements and *Hacked Again* book signings, I enjoy surveying audiences around the country to take their collective cybersecurity pulse. One constant is the assumption that banks and financial firms are the primary targets for hackers. While these targets are still highly valued by cybercriminals, many are highly fortified and prepared to deal with an array of attacks and compromises. On the other hand, health-care institutions entrusted with protecting hundreds of millions of patients' data are getting increasingly caught with their pants down. Totally unprepared, hospitals continue to fall victim to massive ransomware attacks in 2018 and beyond. A 2018 Ponemon report concluded that

---

64 Steve C. Morgan, "Cybercrime Damages $6 Trillion By 2012," Cybersecurity Ventures, December 7, 2018, https://cybersecurityventures.com/cybercrime-damages-6-trillion-by-2021/.

hospitals have paid up to $408 per compromised record. That's three times higher than any other industry, with no end in sight.[65]

In mid-2014, just three months after the Anthem breach occurred, hackers compromised the networks of Premera Blue Cross to snatch eleven million applicants' and members' personal, medical, and financial records. This breach wasn't actually discovered until January 2015. And who knows how many more breaches will be publicly revealed in the health-care sector alone?

BEST PRACTICES MUST ACTUALLY BE PRACTICED

Going forward, health-care organizations stand to gain insight from Anthem's failures as both a cautionary tale and a what-not-to-do procedural. Since the breach initially began with a phishing email opened by a low-level employee, it truly underscores the importance of best practices implemented throughout the entire organization. Best practices start with education and testing of cybersecurity awareness of all, but this is just part of prevention, which is an ongoing lesson. I recommend security awareness professionals like www.KnowBe4.com for comprehensive cybersecurity training. The company's core focus is raising cybersecurity awareness so that employees alter their behaviors and question suspicious activities before it's too late.

After the Anthem investigation was complete, it was determined the attack was probably launched by a nation-

65   Seth Rosenblatt and Pinguino Kolb, "Ransomware Attacks Against Hospitals: A Timeline," The Parallax, September 18, 2018, https://the-parallax.com/2018/09/18/hospital-ransomware-attacks-timeline/.

state attacker, but no specific country has been indicated to date. We can count on the fact that the end of health-care breaches is not in sight. That leaves hospitals, urgent care facilities, insurers, physical therapy and addiction treatment centers, and other small businesses in desperate need of prevention before they become the next Anthem.

 POP QUIZ:
What is the best way to keep employees from falling for phishing scams?

A. Email filters that block suspicious attachments.

B. Cybersecurity awareness training.

C. Pop-up blockers.

Part 3: The Future of Cybersecurity

CHAPTER 19

The Battle over Our Data Has Just Begun

One of the largest data privacy battles between tech giant Apple and the FBI played out for the world following the horrific 2015 San Bernardino terrorist attack. Consumers, techies, tech companies, and world governments were all interested because they could be affected by the rulings. Big tech and data companies have clashed with superpower governments in the past, but those showdowns typically ended with hefty fines being levied against those companies. This situation was different because it felt like everything was on the line. The richest company in the world was pitted against its own wealthiest home country over its citizens' right to privacy balanced against law enforcement's right to easily collect evidence to prevent terrorism.

It seemed that everyone had an opinion. The only problem was that there were so many layers to this particular argument that most opinions were aligned with a basic misunderstanding of the facts, technology, and events. Here is a short list of opinions and arguments I fielded during this time:

- "Apple should just hand over the data to the FBI."
- "The FBI just wants a master key for all of our data."
- "Companies like Apple are making Americans unsafe."
- "Why can't the encryption on the terrorist's iPhone be broken just this once?"
- "I refuse to support a company that breaks the law and defies the US government."
- "I support Apple because they are the only ones trying to keep our data private and secure."

I suppose there are kernels of truth to be found within each of these statements, but this story seemed to force even casual observers to take a side. If this controversy wasn't already everyone's business, it certainly feels as if it should be.

The central dispute concerns the extent to which US courts can compel mobile phone manufacturers like Apple to assist in unlocking smartphones to access potential terrorist-related data when the contents are protected by encryption. From the consumers' perspective, there is a perceived privacy standard in place. When a mobile phone user talks, texts, or emails, that content is thought to be private. Of course, much of this perception changed after whistleblower Edward Snowden revealed much of the NSA's mass surveillance on US and non-US citizens, particularly their cell phones.

THE ALL WRITS ACT

Laws do not always keep up with technology, and in the Apple vs. FBI / San Bernardino iPhone 5c scenario, many questions arose about whether the laws needed to be updated to meet current technology. In 2015 and 2016, Apple received a total of eleven orders issued by the US district courts under the All Writs Act.[66] This law the courts referenced was adopted back in 1789—long before smartphones but not before secret codes and even thoughts. Currently, the US government has the right to seize documents and data but does not have the right to compel citizens to incriminate themselves by revealing data or passwords. This right, also known as the fifth amendment, was coincidentally added to the US Constitution in the same year as the All Writs Act.

---

66 Wikipedia, s.v. "FBI–Apple encryption dispute," updated April 14, 2019, https://en.wikipedia.org/wiki/FBI–Apple_encryption_dispute

The US Supreme Court ruled that federal administrative agencies can invoke the All Writs Act to preserve the status quo when a party within the agency's jurisdiction is about to take action that will prevent or impair the agency from carrying out its functions. This vague and antiquated law gives law enforcement broad powers over our personal data. The US government has revived the All Writs Act in the past decade, most notably to gain access to password-protected mobile phones in domestic terrorism and narcotics investigations. Since 2008, the government has been trying to use the All Writs Act to force tech companies to provide assistance in cracking their customers' smartphones. The American Civil Liberties Union (ACLU) has confirmed seventy-six cases in twenty-two states where the government applied for an order under the All Writs Act.[67]

On February 16, 2016, the FBI invoked the All Writs Act in an order that would force Apple to create a special version of its iOS operating system. This proposed special iOS version would include a security "backdoor" allowing the FBI unfettered access to any confiscated phone— potentially hundreds of millions of phones, including ones just like the iPhone 5c seized in the 2015 San Bernardino terrorist attack. This access would still be granted on a case-by-case basis with properly issued warrants by judges, but as we've seen in many terrorist-related cases, rationale and motives are highly subjective in such politically charged cases.

---

67 Wikipedia, s.v. "All Writs Act," updated March 17, 2019, https://en.wikipedia.org/wiki/All_Writs_Act.

APPLE WEIGHS IN

Then FBI Director James Comey specifically requested that Apple disable the iPhone's feature that erases encrypted data on the device after ten incorrect password attempts. Apple claimed that complying with the order would make brute-force password attacks trivial for anyone with access to a phone using this software. In an open letter, Apple CEO Tim Cook warned of the precedent that following such an order would create. On the same day, leading nonprofit digital privacy and free speech organization EFF (Electronic Frontier Foundation) announced its support for Apple's position along with several public figures, including other tech giants Google, Microsoft, and Facebook. Even Edward Snowden implored Google to side with Apple, stating, "This is the most important tech case in a decade. Silence means Google picked a side, but it's not the public's."[68] The terrorists had struck more than year earlier, but the public war on privacy vs. security had just begun.

Strong opinions on both sides fueled a national conversation that needed to be discussed. On February 17, 2016, I weighed in on NBC4 Los Angeles with my two cents, stating, "Apple agreeing to comply with the court order would be a very slippery slope, and all our personal data would be in jeopardy." On that same day, Tim Cook appeared on the CBS news program *60 Minutes* and emphasized that the only way to protect consumers' personal data is through encryption. As a longtime Apple

---

68   Jose Pagliery, "Edward Snowden Defends Apple in Fight Against FBI," CNN Business, February 17, 2016, https://money.cnn.com/2016/02/17/technology/apple-fbi-phone-unlock-edward-snowden/.

fan and strong privacy advocate, my views seemed to align with both Apple's and the tech industry as a whole.

Of course, not everyone was happy with Apple's position. Senator John McCain went on to make veiled threats against Cook and other Silicon Valley CEOs for not complying with the FBI's requests. But at the end of the day, Apple did not break any laws or even defy any laws. The company appealed a court order that would unlock one iPhone because, as they argued it, it could apply to millions of other iPhones. Apple's contention was seen by many as nothing more than self-serving and marketing speak, but I believe privacy was at the crux of the matter.

ENCRYPTION
Digital encryption has been widely used in many forms of security for decades. And while all encryption is mathematically perfect and strong encryption (128-bit or more) requires some supercomputers years to crack, data will always be vulnerable to some points of attack. This fact necessitates strong encryption on any device users want to protect from rogue hackers, enemy agents, and even our own government. In as far as law enforcement cannot compel US citizens to testify or reveal their own passwords, encryption is simply another means to facilitate this right to privacy.

But Apple and the FBI were never truly at odds. Apple has complied with authorities many times by handing over legally warranted data evidence. Sure, it wanted different rulings from the judge overseeing this particular case, but both parties were indirectly angling for the same thing: a legal precedent on the value of our digital data. Until there is a ruling by the US Supreme Court or Congress passes legislation defining encryption use and repercussions, this issue will continue to rise and fall with the tide of security. It already has.

Just a little over a month after reaching the full boiling point, the FBI withdrew its case against Apple and rumors instantly began to emerge over the reasons. At the time, it was believed that Cellebrite—an Israeli company known for hacking impenetrable smartphone security, including Apple's latest iOS—had sold an obscure method for cracking the phones to the FBI. Since then, Cellebrite has denied these rumors, but the fact remains that someone taught the FBI how to crack an iPhone 5c. Perhaps it was the NSA.

When I speak of "cracking" an iPhone or other devices, I am not referring to breaking any encryption. Even with the most advanced technology, mathematically breaking strong encryption borders on the impossible. Cracking devices like encrypted iPhones generally relies on known exploits that can bypass certain security measures. The most common target is the number of PIN-entry retries allowed before the phone's OS locks out all attempts. If you have only ten chances to enter the right PIN, you had better have the correct PIN already figured out. But if you have millions of chances to enter the correct PIN, you can afford to try every possible variation until the device unlocks.

Cellebrite was believed to be exploiting something along that line, which is why it was approached by the FBI to unlock the terrorist's iPhone 5c at the center of all the controversy. Unfortunately, all of that attention can sometimes attract the wrong people. In early 2017, according to the Motherboard website, Cellebrite itself was hacked and relieved of approximately 900 GB of its mobile forensic customer data.[69] Cellebrite claimed the database was old and that the company had already migrated to a newer, more secure system, but any hacker can see the value of a long list of law enforcement and government agencies looking to crack open mobile devices.

Cellebrite reportedly charges $5,000 to unlock an iPhone, but other services have surfaced, including GrayShift, a company specializing in hacking iPhones with a hardware device it sells to law enforcement. These black boxes are called GrayKey and sell for $15,000 to unlock up to three hundred devices and $30,000 for an unlimited number of unlocks to law enforcement agencies. Since GrayKey relies on iOS security exploits, they are effective only if the iPhone does not have the latest iOS security update patches. Hackers always seem to find their way around encrypted data, while governments still believe they have the right to any encryption keys.

AUSTRALIA LEADS THE WAY

After months of resistance from tech companies, the Australian government forged ahead and made good on its threats to pass anti-encryption legislation in early 2019. This new legislation not only arms law enforcement agents with more surveillance power but also disarms tech companies in their efforts to provide better privacy and security to

---

69   Joseph Cox, "Hacker Steals 900 GB of Cellebrite Data," Motherboard, January 12, 2017, https://motherboard.vice.com/en_us/article/3daywj/hacker-steals-900-gb-of-cellebrite-data.

their customers. Australia's new Assistance and Access Bill 2018 compels companies to hand over all requested user data.[70] Tech companies have been complying for years when legal warrants were presented and will continue to do so. However, this law also includes end-to-end encrypted data. Such data cannot be provided unless each company provides a "backdoor" solution or key to law enforcement, essentially breaking encryption. This hurt tech companies that have built business models on protecting their customers' privacy; it only makes criminals, terrorists, and anyone else requiring absolute privacy seek other means of data protection. But those are just the immediate surface effects.

Australia's new law sends a chilling message to all tech companies. On the surface, individually issued decryption keys might sound like a fair compromise or at least a necessary evil. But to the average cybersecurity expert or engineer, the same people tasked with securing our data and privacy, this is a disaster in the making. Putting aside the abuses of power, IP theft, state-sponsored spying, and over-all hacking that will likely all proliferate once any decryption key is created, regular users can never have total privacy again. We've already seen warrantless law enforcement abuses from local police all the way up to massive NSA spying programs. Those abuses of power or sanctioned hacks cannot occur when data is encrypted. Once we're prepared to hand our innermost secrets to our government and leave

---

70   Mariella Moon, "Australia's Controversial Anti-Encryption Bill Passes into Law," Engadget, December 7, 2018, https://www.engadget.com/2018/12/07/australia-accessassistance-bill-now-a-law/.

personal privacy behind, we have left the United States and entered into a land somewhere between China's socialist republic and George Orwell's fictional Oceania from *1984*, his seminal novel.

THE BACKLASH

In response to Australia's new legislation, Apple, Dropbox, Evernote, Facebook, Google, LinkedIn, Microsoft, Oath, Snapchat, and Twitter have penned a letter of protest entitled "Reform Government Surveillance." This letter claims that the new mandate seeks to "undermine the cybersecurity, human rights, or the right to privacy of our users."[71] These tech giants are primarily concerned with preserving their business models and revenue projections, but that doesn't mean they don't want to protect their users' privacy and data integrity as well. When governments seek to weaken encryption, privacy is the first casualty.

 POP QUIZ:
What is the best way to maintain privacy between two parties?

    A. Long and strong passwords and two-factor authentication.

    B. Encrypted cloud services.

    C. End-to-end encryption.

---

71   Andrew Couts, "Google, Microsoft, Apple, and More Launch 'Reform Government Surveillance' Campaign," Digital Trends, December 9, 2018, https://www.digitaltrends.com/web/tech-giants-launch-reform-government-surveillance-campaign/.

CHAPTER 20

Crypto Capitalism

The US dollar has survived world wars, recessions, depressions, and market crashes for over two hundred years. Since 1775, the US Federal Reserve has seen to the dollar's health and well-being with approximately $1.5 trillion in circulation as of 2017.[72] But the dollar's gold-standard status is being challenged by another new high-tech currency contender almost every day. Cryptocurrency promises the security of credit with

---

72   Mitchell Hartman, "How Much Money Is There in the World?" Marketplace, October 30, 2017, https://www.marketplace.org/2017/10/30/world/how-much-money-there-world.

all the anonymity of cash in one unified system, but how can this new form of digital currency benefit your small business and your wallet?

USES OF CRYPTOCURRENCY

Cryptocurrency is digital currency and can also be thought of as "virtual" money. Bitcoin is the most popular form of cryptocurrency, but there are dozens of competing standards that differ in both subtle and major ways. Due to Bitcoin's popularity, I will be using terms like Bitcoin and cryptocurrency interchangeably, but just know that there are many other cryptocurrencies in use.

Most consumers aren't aware of the fact that since 1971, US citizens have been able to utilize Federal Reserve notes as a form of money without any gold or silver backing. So if you opened your wallet some fifty years ago and pulled out a dollar bill, you would've seen: "THIS NOTE IS LEGAL TENDER FOR ALL DEBTS, PUBLIC AND PRIVATE, AND IS REDEEMABLE IN LAWFUL MONEY AT THE UNITED STATES TREASURY OR AT ANY FEDERAL RESERVE BANK."

But pull out any dollar bill today and you will see: "THIS NOTE IS LEGAL TENDER FOR ALL DEBTS, PUBLIC AND PRIVATE." In other words, you can't redeem it for "lawful" money anymore—meaning currency backed by gold and silver.

The US government can print only so much money out of thin air and wants you to believe that our country's gross domestic product (GDP) is still backing the dollar and providing stability. But if government spending continues to run the show, there will be a wakeup call at some point. As consumers continue to borrow and accrue more debt (credit cards, mortgages, and small loans), they only fall deeper into debt with less of a chance to climb back out as each day passes. Similarly, as the US government continues to outspend its GDP, it will eventually default on big loans with other sovereign nations (we have borrowed the most from China), and when those nations come collecting, disagreements might quickly turn into full-scale wars. As of June 2019, the US national debt has reached a whopping $22.4 trillion, but the real problems began back in 2008 with the US banking crisis. So what can you do when faith in centralized banking institutions fall to an all-time low? You create a new currency.

BITCOIN
You can't physically hold a Bitcoin or hand it to a retailer anymore than you can pay for lunch with gold bullion. Bitcoin is an electronic peer-to-peer payment system alternative to brick-and-mortar banking. Since all exchanges are made via digital-wallet software with no central bank or authority, the value is derived from pure market supply and demand. Other digital payment systems, such as PayPal, Venmo, and Apple Pay, still rely on traditional banks to regulate interest rates, supply, and demand in order to stabilize currency. If you've followed Bitcoin's meteoric rise and fall throughout 2018, you know that stability is not one its selling points—more on that later.

The Bitcoin supply is finite. Production of Bitcoin is referred to as "mining" with every transaction, using extremely complex algorithms and a network of computers and "miners" essentially competing against one another. When a miner successfully verifies the completion of these cryptographic "puzzles," they are awarded a small amount of Bitcoin. This is how new Bitcoins are introduced into the blockchain system.

The blockchain is simply a cryptographically secure ledger of every single Bitcoin creation and transaction that every single peer (as in peer-to-peer) must agree on—simple in theory, but here's the rub: the algorithm puzzle used to create each Bitcoin becomes more complex each and every time a new Bitcoin enters into the blockchain. This means that even though Bitcoin value fluctuates in the marketplace of transactions, the time, energy, and ultimately value of every Bitcoin is increased due to a reduced supply. The theoretical number of Bitcoins that can exist is limited to twenty-one million as the production rate is halved every four years to ensure that the value of a Bitcoin is not lost. By 2140, the supply of Bitcoin is expected to run dry. At that time, miners will no longer be rewarded with new Bitcoins but instead will be paid for their efforts in transaction fees.

However, some miners want to have their cake and eat it too. This is when dishonest crypto miners effectively team up against the honest miners in an effort to collect a "double spend." A double spend is like writing a bad check, but that can happen only if the blockchain is split at just the right moment by 51 percent of the mining pool. Until recently, this known vulnerability was only a hypothetical and known as the "51 percent attack" or when an individual miner or group of miners could control more than 50 percent of a network's mining. But in early 2019, Coinbase, a digital currency exchange headquartered in San Francisco, reported on a very real occurrence in an Ethereum cryptocurrency spinoff. Miners were able to sell Ethereum coins for cash and then alter the blockchain ledger in such a way that allowed them to retain their sold coins and also walk away with the cash. Hackers were able to bilk the Ethereum Classic blockchain out of $1 million spread across twenty transactions.[73] This fundamental blockchain weakness was first described by Satoshi Nakamoto, the purported creator of Bitcoin, when he or she first described blockchain's overreliance on a critical mass of "honest" miners in order stop double spending.[74] This is one of the few advantages that centralized banks continue to hold over Bitcoin, but that hasn't dissuaded cryptocurrency enthusiasts.

Of course, this assumes people will still care about and use Bitcoin in the future. With so many other cryptocurrencies on the market and Bitcoin's volatility, it's nearly impossible to predict any cryptocurrency's place in our economy five years from now, much less in one hundred years. Back in late 2017, Bitcoin speculation was all the rage, and I was no exception. I did a live segment with Cheddar TV on the floor of the NYSE in which I talked about cryptocurrency ecosystems and how hackers target

---

73 Mike Orcutt, "Hackers May Have Just Stolen $1 Million from the Ethereum Classic Blockchain in a '51%' Attack," *MIT Technology Review*, January 8, 2019, https://www.technologyreview.com/f/612728/hackers-just-stole-1-million-from-the-ethereum-classic-blockchain-in-a-rare-51/.

74 Satoshi Nakamoto, "Bitcoin: A Peer-to-Peer Electronic Cash System," Bitcoin.com, October 31, 2008, https://www.bitcoin.com/bitcoin.pdf.

the exchanges and wallets rather than actually hacking Bitcoin itself. I was also asked to share my predictions on when the Bitcoin bubble might burst. My unofficial guess on the Bitcoin ceiling was around $20,000 and at that time, Bitcoin just broke into the $17,000 range. By December 16, 2017, Bitcoin had surged to $19,343 (just shy of my $20,000 prediction) only to reverse and steadily plummet to under $4,000 by the end of 2018.

While I continue to work with firms launching initial coin offerings (ICOs) and blockchain technology and follow the market myself, I have never purchased—and don't plan to—any Bitcoins due to the issues. ICOs are used to fund the development of new cryptocurrencies. Investors are typically offered units of the new cryptocurrency in exchange against other cryptocurrencies such as Bitcoin.

THE BITCOIN "MINERS" AND LIMITED RESOURCES

Globally, there is a network of mining computers over 250 times more powerful than the world's top five hundred supercomputers combined. Since GPU-intensive mining "rigs" require so much processing power, electricity becomes its own form of currency to be resold, borrowed, or stolen by miners just like Bitcoins are. According to a recent report by *Xin'an Evening News*, the Chinese police discovered a Bitcoin mining farm in Bengbu in the Anhui Province when the local electric power company saw a huge spike in electricity consumption. The power company saw surges as high as 97 percent where it would normally reach only 5 percent. After an inspection of household power meters, authorities discovered suspicious power cables attached to the power box of an industrial building. These cables were traced back to a particular residence in which fifty Bitcoin miners were found working.[75]

It is estimated that a single Bitcoin transaction currently requires electricity comparable to the daily consumption of 1.6 American households. This energy requirement will only continue to rise as the Bitcoin algorithms increase in complexity. Therefore, it becomes clear that adopting Bitcoin as a major global currency would needlessly increase energy consumption beyond our capabilities. Bitcoin is not just energy dependent for each transaction but also to create each Bitcoin. An estimated thirty tera-watt hours were used to mine Bitcoins in 2017, which is

---

75   Red Li, "Illegal Bitcoin Mining Farm Cracked Down by Chinese Police," 8BTC, December 14, 2016, https://news.8btc.com/illegal-bitcoin-mining-farm-cracked-down-by-chinese-police.

approximately the same energy used to power all of Ireland in that same year.[76]

But power theft is not the only victim of Bitcoin's power-hungry mining needs. Nvidia, a leading maker of GPUs for PCs around the world, saw its stock rise in lockstep with Bitcoin's gains and subsequently fall too. Since Bitcoin mining is so reliant on powerful GPUs, Nvidia enjoyed a new profit center from cryptocurrency miners running hundreds of GPU rigs in their garages 24-7. As the Bitcoin market began to fall away from these digital speculators, they responded by sharply cutting orders for Nvidia GPUs, so the market responded with Nvidia shares dropping to nearly one half of its former glory in only two months.

CRYPTOMANIA

Nevertheless, "cryptomania" continues all over social media and traditional media and even with established investors. By the end of 2017, the SEC chairman issued warnings to investors about deals that may be too good to be true.[77] Unfortunately, many companies have jumped on the crypto bandwagon by using their smoke and mirrors to lure unsuspecting investors into the magical world of cryptocurrency. Like the stock market, greed, fear, and strong emotions rule cryptoinvestments, but at least the stock market is regulated and has oversight. Publicly traded

---

76   Alex Horn, "Bitcoin Mining Consumes More Electricity a Year Than Ireland," *Guardian*, November 27, 2017, https://www.theguardian.com/technology/2017/nov/27/bitcoin-mining-consumes-electricity-ireland.

77   Jeff John Roberts, "The SEC Chair's Cryptocurrency Warning: 5 Things to Know," *Fortune*, December 12, 2017, https://fortune.com/2017/12/12/cryptocurrency-blockchain-ico-sec/.

corporations have tangible assets and business disclosures that allow investors to place a level of confidence in what they are buying into. Private ICOs and cryptocurrency investments do not fall under the same scrutiny, so I urge all potential investors to stop and reconsider before diving in headfirst. Putting the investment risks aside, there are still major security issues with cryptocurrencies like Bitcoin. So how are Bitcoins stolen when cryptocurrency's biggest selling point is security?

CRYPTOTHEFT

In February 2014, Mt. Gox, a Tokyo-based Bitcoin exchange that was once the largest of its kind, was forced into bankruptcy protection due to Bitcoin being hacked. Back in 2011, a company auditor's computer led hackers straight into the exchange, where they proceeded to artificially alter the price of Bitcoin, transfer Bitcoins from customer accounts, and then sell them for a huge profit. When it was discovered, Mt. Gox suspended trading, but it was already too late. They lost $450 million, and of the 2,000 Bitcoins that were initially transferred and sold, 650 were never returned.

Thus began the distrust of cryptocurrency by some countries. Thailand was the first to completely ban several cryptocurrencies as a means to invest in ICOs, and China followed by banning banks from trading Bitcoins at the end of 2013. However, such bans serve more to protect exchanges and their users from being hacked rather than the entire cryptocurrency system. When a brick-and-mortar bank is robbed, the thieves do not compromise the US Mint in any way. The same holds true when a crypto exchange is hacked. Users might lose millions and the exchange could even go under, but this has nothing to do with the blockchain protocol itself. However, unlike traditional banks being subject to FDIC rules, a crypto exchange does not live by the same set of rules and precautions, so customers have no guarantees of safety and are unprotected should a crypto exchange fall prey to hackers, for example.

There is a growing trend to hijack computers by using CPU and GPU processor cycles to mine Bitcoins surreptitiously. Source code has appeared on numerous websites and within apps planted without the user's knowledge and sometimes without the app owner's knowledge. Since crypto mining operations are computationally intensive processes, work that can be distributed across a network of thousands or even millions of devices greatly increases the speed at which Bitcoins can be mined. Since WordPress websites make up nearly one third of the internet, they have become the primary targets. Like millions of Android smartphones, millions of WordPress sites are not maintained properly with recent security updates. These soft targets allow hackers and miners to steal CPU and GPU cycles in the background for mining without the user's knowledge. The only indications might manifest as poorer performance and quicker battery discharge rates for infected mobile devices.

FUTURE OF CRYPTOCURRENCY

As Bitcoin and other cryptocurrencies enter into future markets and become more widely accepted, they will likely continue to fluctuate. These surges in value attract hackers who capitalize on cryptocurrency hacking by stealing and then cashing out on the upswing. The funny thing is that most of the millions of stolen Bitcoins are now nearly worthless when compared to the height of the bubble or when they were mostly stolen. So unlike a dollar that was a dollar fifty years ago and continues to be a dollar to this day, a Bitcoin is just a fraction of the value it held not too long ago. Of course, Bitcoin could always rally again, but in the meantime, I enjoy a perverse pleasure in knowing that cyberthieves are frustrated by their substantially less valuable booty. Since cryptocurrencies are challenging for law enforcement to track and provide a powerful level of anonymity, hackers will continue to gravitate toward those digital currencies.

Newer cryptocurrencies offer significantly faster and cheaper transaction fees, but for criminals, anonymity has always been the prime reason to use Bitcoin in the first place. Since so many hackers have turned to Bitcoin, law enforcement has intensified its efforts and methods to catch these criminals. Within Bitcoin's blockchain, every user needs a public address of numbers and letters in order to receive payments. Law enforcement and intelligence agencies can effectively track the movement of funds and isolate these public addresses to specific hackers. So when the criminals try to cash out at a traditional bank or a regulated entity, they can be caught. Therefore, many criminals have been shifting away from Bitcoin and onto other digital currencies that are still new and more challenging for law enforcement to track.

All criminal activity using various cryptocurrencies is hard to track, but some estimate that Bitcoin use has steadily declined as the go-to digital currency across the Dark Web. Overall, digital currency transaction volume for illegal activity is on the rise, but not all cryptocurrency is the same. Many hackers are gravitating toward other cryptocurrencies, such as Zcash and Monero, since they have additional cryptographic features that make transactions even more challenging for law enforcement to detect. Bitcoin mining malware is also not as popular as other cryptocurrency because the more popular Bitcoin becomes, the harder its algorithms are to mine.

TRADING IN BITCOIN

Bitcoin might be fighting to maintain its place as the top cryptocurrency, but you can already obtain Bitcoins at specific ATM locations. A great resource to find over one thousand Bitcoin ATMs globally—with more than five hundred US locations alone—is www.coinatmradar.com. The website provides the physical address, rates, and any applicable transaction fees. Most of those ATMs even allow you to buy and sell Bitcoins on the spot.

Trading Bitcoins requires some advanced technical knowledge and is more often accomplished through third parties who effectively manage trades through the exchanges and digital wallets software. There are two types of digital wallets: a cold wallet and a hot wallet. A "cold wallet" stores cryptocurrency offline because it is not connected to the internet. This kind of storage protects the wallet from unauthorized access that can occur only when connected to the internet. A cold wallet can be likened to a savings account or even a credit card due to the extra layers of security that somewhat obfuscate the funds from hackers. A "hot wallet" is cryptographically protected but always connected to the internet. It is much more convenient for smaller, more frequent cryptocurrency transactions. I would liken it to a checking account or debit card that delivers fast transactions but with fewer security measures in place in case something goes wrong.

Conventional markets are unstable enough right now, so speculating on the future of any cryptocurrency feels like an exercise in futility. Many well-meaning cryptocurrency investors and entrepreneurs have lost and will continue to lose their shirts and that doesn't even include losses exceeding $1.7 billion just due to misplaced or forgotten passwords and theft.[78] It takes only a few clever hackers to score big and scare off mainstream adoption, ruining it for everyone else. On the other hand, the big players in the world economy are no strangers to wild fluctuations regularly breaking into the trillions of dollars. As we saw back in 2008, the crashing economies that gave birth to Bitcoin and the potential of a decentralized cryptocurrency could easily double down and give rise to a newer digital currency standard. Like any first-generation product, Bitcoin could serve as version 1.0 for its first decade of life and then evolve into a newer, more robust and accepted standard.

---

78   Gertrude Chavez-Dreyfuss, "Cryptocurrency Thefts, Scams Hit $1.7 Billion in 2018: Report," Reuters, January 29, 2019, https://www.reuters.com/article/us-crypto-currency-crime/cryptocurrency-thefts-scams-hit-1-7-billion-in-2018-report-idUSKCN1PN1SQ.

POP QUIZ:
Which of the following cryptocurrency statements is false:

A. Blockchain is the digital ledger that records all cryptocurrency transactions.

B. Each new Bitcoin mined requires slightly more energy than the previous one.

C. Cryptocurrency is one hundred times more secure than traditional currency.

CHAPTER 21

Airborne Threats

In the case of drone technology, it's not a matter of *if* but simply a matter of *when*. When what? you may ask. Drones and unmanned aerial vehicles (UAVs) hold tremendous potential to enhance consumer and industrial marketplaces. We've all seen the Amazon drone delivery concept videos, but eventually these will be seen as quaint technological artifacts from the recent past. Like a grainy film from the 1950s that predicts jetliner air travel for all with the comforts and conveniences of home, the current drone videos appeal to those same sensibilities of advancement and betterment of society.

Step outside and gaze to the sky long enough. Perhaps you will see a few airliners streak by at forty thousand feet overhead. Stare long enough and you might even see a tiny consumer drone flitter by. Now jump ten years into the future. It's projected that we will be subjected to low-altitude air traffic as far as the eye can see. Swarms of tiny and medium-sized drones will blanket the skies in regular intervals, similar to highway traffic patterns, but without the jams and irregular stops and starts associated with drivers.

Since this air traffic will be relatively low, between four hundred and five hundred feet from the ground, it will live in a space low enough not to disrupt large passenger and freight air travel and high enough not to disrupt life on the ground. Of course, city areas with tall buildings and large towers will be taken into account but not by an air traffic controller sitting in a radar-guided tower somewhere. The *A* in UAV is the truly autonomous part and also the traditional definition of a drone. That will be monitored and controlled in the cloud, both literally and figuratively.

DRONE TECHNOLOGY

All drones use their built-in sensors to determine speed, position, and distance relative to their destinations and other nearby drones. This local sensory data is useful to each and every drone, but it is much more useful to the AI-powered air traffic controller in the cloud. When it comes to drone traffic, this system will be all knowing and all seeing. Much more than just a dumb traffic light, the system will use combinations of LIDAR, RF wireless, infrared, and other imaging data to navigate millions of flying drones simultaneously. Just think of such a system as the ultimate traffic cop, but instead of simply directing commuters to stop or go, this traffic cop would seize total control over your vehicle for the entire duration of your journey. Unlike most self-driving automobile network proposals, drone networks tend to undergo more scrutiny because of the inherent fear of heavy objects falling out of the sky and onto people due to a rogue drone pilot.

Nearly instant deliveries, personal air transportation, and real-time continuous monitoring of the globe are just three huge markets that should change our lives for the better. But this is a cybersecurity book, so not only am I going to discuss the downside of drones, I'm going to tell you why drones scare me more than any other cybersecurity threat.

Hacking is achieved in many forms. Popular TV depictions of cybercrime from *Black Mirror* to *Mr. Robot* might lead one to assume that all hackers remotely break into computer networks and hold companies hostage for their data. This stereotype holds true in most cases because it's simply safer, more convenient, and more secure for virtual intruders to case a joint and make off with the goods from the comfort of their own homes. Physical presence is something reserved for the truly daring hackers. So the proliferation of drones comes at an auspicious time during this steep rise in the general incidence of hacking.

HACKING THE DRONES

In some ways, drones are the logical extension of the hacker's turf. And while not all devices are buzzing and hovering over their targets, CCTV cameras, mobile devices, and network switches can act as proxies for the eyes and ears of omniscient intruders. They help feed the senses that ultimately exploit their victims, but why should any hacker be content with fixed devices they do not directly control?

Enter the drone. UAVs, quadcopters, UAS—whatever term is used, it always refers to an unmanned flying vehicle that is either fully or partially autonomous. And since hackers are continually innovating their approaches, infected USB sticks no longer rate high in the hacker's arsenal. They want something even more ubiquitous to spread malware. The proliferation of smartphones, Bluetooth, NFC, and Wi-Fi hotspots offer hackers numerous attack points. Wireless threats, such as the infamous KRACK Wi-Fi vulnerability—which was discovered in 2016 and allows hackers to easily see unencrypted Wi-Fi traffic but not your password—can exploit millions of unprotected devices using WPA2. These devices, especially the older ones, still tend to be in operation and are found in cheaper electronic appliances, routers, and even drones. So not only can drones be used for spying and malware delivery, they can also be the target of malicious attacks for said purposes and much more.

POTENTIAL THREATS

Back in 2011, I received a call from a Department of Homeland Security (DHS) agent at a mobile command center based in Texas. He asked whether my company offered tools that could detect drone threats. Since we had been selling wireless threat-detection tools to government agencies for some time, his query wasn't completely out of the blue, but I didn't have any solutions ready to go. Still, I was curious about his application. The agent explained that there was a credible threat to large stadiums involving drones that could cause significant harm to spectators.

Anytime I hear someone define a wireless security problem, my mind races to see if a solution aligns with the engineering expertise of my company, BVS. In this case, it sounded like a good fit. At that time, consumer drones were beginning to appear over all kinds of public places for mostly benign reasons, but there was a growing concern that wireless networks could be compromised and public safety communications disrupted. Another less likely scenario involved drones coupled with firearms or small payloads of explosives. He mentioned they had no means of identifying a small drone target other than visually, and by then it's usually too late. The DHS mobile command center wanted not only an early warning alert to approaching drones but also a way to quickly hunt down the pilot.

My RF engineering team quickly realized that most low-cost consumer drones utilized off-the-shelf Wi-Fi chips and protocols that we could already monitor. BVS has been selling advanced Wi-Fi spectrum and demodulation tools for professional installers since 1999, so we modified our Wi-Fi sniffing tools by adding drone detection. This allowed law enforcement agents to uniquely identify the drone make and model and its associated statistics, such as speed, altitude, range, and run time. And since we were locking onto the drone's Wi-Fi MAC address, we could utilize our direction-finding antenna to detect the drone *before* it was visible to the eye. Note that machine access control (MAC) is the unique device identifier assigned to every Wi-Fi device.

This lock we had on every Wi-Fi packet would also allow agents to "see" and hunt down the pilot controlling that drone in flight. Of course, sophisticated drone manufacturers like DJI.com have introduced models using proprietary wireless video links and telemetry that do not share any Wi-Fi protocols, so they would fall outside our ability to detect. But the scope of our solution still covered the overwhelming majority of consumer drones on the market at that time.

In June 2015, I was asked to testify as a cybersecurity expert alongside members of the Academy of Model Aeronautics (AMA) before the Assembly Homeland Security and State Preparedness Committee of the New Jersey State Legislature in Trenton on credible threats that drones pose to critical infrastructure, such as the electric power grids. The committee was preparing to vote on proposed legislation that "Establishes fourth degree crime of conducting surveillance of critical infrastructures using drones and requires certain drones to be registered and insured."

I spent the better part of two hours explaining both the worst-case scenarios and some more likely scenarios of a drone being used as a weapon. I even brought along one of the most advanced consumer drones at the time, a DJI Inspire 1, and its pilot to hover in the Trenton State House for a few minutes to wow the crowd. I've done dozens of live cybersecurity presentations, so I knew the best way to wake up a weary cybersecurity audience was to bring out the drone. More so than any celebrity appearance, flying drones, especially indoors, get the audience's attention and usually result in hundreds of smartphone pics and tweets. And as far as I know and was told, this was the first flying drone to christen the third-oldest (built in 1790) state house in continuous legislative use in the United States.

Hopefully, the brief spectacle didn't overshadow the important messages I was trying to impart. The AMA representatives in attendance were particularly interested in ensuring the public safety of airline passengers, along with compliance from their large membership of remote airplane, helicopter, and drone pilots. Increased incidents of drone collisions with full-size aircraft had risen, but that was not my primary concern. I found myself taking the presentation down a much darker road, more resembling the next 9/11.

I shared my wireless expertise and posed a credible terrorist scenario involving multiple drones equipped with explosives flown below radar near a nuclear facility. There are multiple critical infrastructure weak points in any nuclear facility, but the ones I highlighted could be taken out with drones and even lead to full meltdown of a nuclear reactor if not secured immediately. Nuclear facilities are always dependent on a steady flow of electricity to keep the reactor's core temperature controlled to prevent a meltdown. Needless to say, I have deliberately left out details, as I am not looking to educate any wannabe hackers and terrorists further. Like terrorism, drones make for great headlines because they are sensationalized by the media and tap into the fear that some forces are entirely out of our control as individuals.

EVEN AT THE WHITE HOUSE

Drones have already caused their share of public panic and even some questionable moments in our national security. On Jan. 27, 2015, a civilian drone breached restricted airspace, crashing onto the White House lawn. Security officials had no way of knowing where it came from or whether it was a credible threat. I fielded many calls that day from news organizations eager to get insight into just what happened, but I had little to offer at the time without any suspects, demands, or threats being made.

The next morning, the drone pilot turned himself in to authorities, but for a moment, the White House and Secret

Service were on full alert, all over a $1,000 consumer drone. The costs associated with national security are unsurprisingly high, but what about the worst-case scenarios? What if this was a terrorist drone dispensing a biological or chemical agent or one strapped with C4 explosives?

All modern drones use an extremely accurate GPS navigation system that can be set to autopilot using waypoints. These navigation systems also contain vulnerabilities that could give a competent hacker access to a drone's data stream or telemetry link connection. Hackers have also demonstrated the ability to spoof the connection between drone and pilot, allowing complete control of the interface. This is similar to common man-in-the-middle attacks targeting mobile devices and computer networks across the internet. Both scenarios pose a credible threat. Drones can be dangerous when carelessly piloted by anyone but even more deadly by terrorists with a little skill.

DRONES AS POTENTIAL WEAPONS

Aircraft of all types have been used as weapons since their introduction. Never was this concept clearer than in the terrorist attacks of 9/11. Of the four commercial airliners that were hijacked, three successfully connected with their targets, killing thousands. This was accomplished through years of planning but ultimately carried out by nineteen hijackers willing to die for their cause. Aside from the jet fuel, these planes had no payload or munitions. The most devastating aspect of the attacks came down to simple choreography between the hijackers. If one flight had struck just a little earlier than the rest of the attackers, all flights could have been grounded and the Federal Aviation Administration (FAA) and US military would have been able to save more lives.

Exchanging those massive planes for tiny, unmanned drones might seem to diminish the damage and casualties from 9/11 attacks, but I don't see it that way. Thanks to the courageous and self-sacrificing efforts of passengers and crew on United Airlines Flight 93, many lives were spared, but that wouldn't have been the case if those planes had been unmanned. Drones are too small for standard radar to distinguish; they can be controlled remotely and even autonomously in the case of swarms. Hundreds of drones could autonomously fly in any formation to their designated targets. They might all carry payloads of explosives or biowarfare agents, or perhaps just one does. How would radar systems that cannot even distinguish between birds and drones possibly identify any of this?

These are genuine fears that inform the security agents who are commissioned to protect all of us. So far, the only headlines involving swarms of drones are relegated to entertainment such as Lady Gaga's Super Bowl halftime performance. Over three hundred drones were programmed by Intel to autonomously fly in the night sky. They created a spectacular light show that culminated in a giant American flag, but the display was not live. That sequence had been taped in advance before the halftime show in order to comply with FAA regulations involving flying drones over crowds. Super Bowl attendees had to watch the light show on the stadium's monitors just like everyone at home.

Since the FAA created the national drone registry in 2013, over forty thousand commercial UAVs have been registered, with no end in sight. These, coupled with the millions of consumer drones already in flight, make for a busy and potentially dangerous sky. We can only hope that our legislation and security efforts keep pace with the rapid advances in autonomous drone technology.

 POP QUIZ:
If you see a suspicious or dangerous drone flying near you, you should:

A. Call the police.

B. Shoot it out of the sky.

C. Call the FAA.

CHAPTER 22

Hacking Planes, Trains, and Automobiles

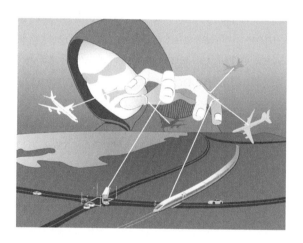

Modern air travel runs the gamut of emotions for all of its passengers. I find travel a forced but welcome downtime to catch up on some reading or watch movies. My wife, however, sees the entire ordeal as a harrowing fear that requires weeks of mental and emotional preparation on her part before the impending flight. But when I'm not admiring the ability of a 175,000-pound steel bird to take flight or the fact that over three hundred thousand such birds do this every single day around the world, I'm left wondering just how safe it truly is. I'm not going to quote you statistics detailing how much safer air travel is than highway travel; I'll save that discussion for my wife. Right now, I want to focus on the critical avionics and navigation systems in all modern airliners.

AIRPLANE VULNERABILITIES

I'll admit that while traveling on a Boeing 737, my cool facade belies a nervous wreck. What if hackers were to start targeting airlines and individual planes by launching ransomware attacks the same way they've already targeted hospitals and police stations? My mind races with nefarious possibilities. They would likely demand a hefty number of anonymous Bitcoins in exchange for returning control back to the pilot. The hackers might even be able to hijack the plane without ever boarding it! Instrumentation, navigation, landing gear, and cabin pressurization are all vulnerable to hackers; my worries tailspin out of control and my gaze locks onto my in-flight entertainment system before me. But this same in-flight entertainment system has been demonstrated to be a security weakness of this very airplane by a colleague of mine.

In 2015, security researcher Chris Roberts created quite a ruckus within the media, FBI, FAA, and fellow hackers when he casually tweeted about hacking a 737 he was traveling on at the time. Of course, his tweet was more satire than reality, but his point was to raise legitimate safety concerns by calling attention to them in a public forum. Chris got more than he bargained for when he was booted off that plane for his tweet, though, and had his laptop confiscated and searched while questioned by the FBI for four hours. Even though Chris is a white hat security expert with a long-standing record of professional research, his claim seemed to have irked the wrong people.

United Airlines immediately contacted the FBI, who met Roberts once the aircraft landed in Syracuse, New York. Chris insisted that he had conducted his past five years of aircraft security research safely and legally, while federal agents claimed a different story of tampering with aircraft electronics. Allegations aside, Chris is a brilliant guy and a valued security researcher. When he appeared on my *What Keeps You Up At Night?* cybersecurity podcast in June 2018, I found Chris engaging, thoughtful, and deeply concerned about the power individual hackers might be able to wield over vast networks of secure and private data. He worried mostly about symbols like the infamous Doomsday Clock and how they fall woefully short in preparing society for catastrophes of all kinds—including compromised air travel, of course.

Since his run-in with the feds, Chris has steered clear of the media spotlight but continues to perform research and speak on a variety of security topics, including airport and aircraft safety. He learned that particular models of aircraft in-flight entertainment systems were connected to the passenger satellite phone network, as well as specific functions used for operating cabin-control systems. In some cases, those systems were even connected to the plane's avionic systems—mistakenly, one would presume. Chris accessed in-flight networks on more than a dozen flights he took but insists he manipulated only simulated flights (he and his colleague changed the engine controls from cruise to climb) and never did anything beyond observing how the data moved through the network to airborne flights.

For some, Chris's research in the wild is too cavalier, but I see his approach as necessary to alert the proper companies and authorities about a lesser-known security flaw. In an interview with *Wired*, Boeing officials deny the possibility of Chris's claims by refuting the idea of two-way communication between any infotainment center and critical navigation systems. Yet *Wired* reporters did discover a document online indicating aircraft support of data buses designed for two-way communications, so hopefully further scrutiny will be applied to these important findings.[79]

TRAIN VULNERABILITIES

Most people don't think of trains as a hackable commodity. Trains lumber along carrying passengers and cargo just as they've done for the last two hundred years. Sure, they are a little faster now and contain electronics, but the service itself hasn't really changed. The US government mandates requiring Positive Train Control (PTC) safety implementation seem to view the modern railway in a similar light. Since 1990, the National Transportation Safety Board (NTSB) has been pushing for some form of PTC, and to date, most railways still have not complied with government mandates. In fact, Congress has pushed the deadline back several times. The latest push allows US railways to operate up until 2020 before steep fines are imposed. PTC is a system of communications between train cars, railways, and railway dispatch centers that is meant to bolster safety, but how does hacking come into play?

Most train accidents are due to some form of human error. Operators face distractions from smartphones,

---

79   Kim Zetter, "Is It Possible for Passengers to Hack Commercial Aircraft?" *Wired*, May 26, 2015, https://www.wired.com/2015/05/possible-passengers-hack-commercial-aircraft/.

dispatchers can suffer from fatigue, and railway inspectors can easily miss minute defects and fractures that can accrue over time. In this age of self-driving cars and jet airliners on autopilot, it's counterintuitive to see trains on tracks as fully operated by people from a journey's start to finish, but that is the case. Since trains still rely heavily on humans to maintain and operate them, they have been slow to upgrade and automate over the years, thereby creating a true conundrum for the railway industry. The archaic mechanical systems of trains rely heavily on humans and the human errors they bring with them. Thus, PTC systems to track and automate safety measures are being slowly but surely integrated around the world. These PTC systems are focused more on physical safety of passengers and the world around them, which is good. However, the lack of focus on system-wide security and privacy is not good. As we now know, any systems involving servers, transponders, and control systems—even closed ones—are vulnerable to hackers.

In a 2015 report, Motherboard detailed the concerns of security researchers over the "lack of authentication protections, systems using very old operating systems, and hard-coded passwords for remote access."[80] These vulnerabilities are reminiscent of concerns over security holes found in older consumer routers and IoT devices. So the more adoption of technology to increase safety and efficiency, the more attacks on security and privacy will

---

80   Joseph Cox, "Security Researchers Offer Warnings About Hackable Railroads," Motherboard, December 27, 2015, https://motherboard.vice.com/en_us/article/gv5bnb/ security-researchers-offer-warnings-about-hackable-railroads-2.

also be likely. In recent years, terrorists have begun to target railways, including those of Spain, Great Britain, and India, by using crude IEDs. Now just imagine the deadly chaos that could be unleashed on network-managed railways and trains around the globe. A simple keystroke could easily send two trains careening into each other at full speed.

As a wireless and cybersecurity expert, I find myself at the crossroads of this dilemma. For several years, my security company has provided thousands of cell-phone-detecting sensors for major railways. These sensors mostly reside on freight cars to detect and alert dispatchers and managers about unauthorized cell phone use by any train operator. The technology continues to be implemented on railways, around mining deposits, and in other operations that require heavy machinery. It is effective and has saved lives, but the security of any system is only as robust as its users. Our cell-phone-detection receivers are not operating on a critical functions network, so a worst-case scenario might involve a hack (usually from a railway employee) that would disable the detector and allow someone to operate an unauthorized smartphone without getting caught by the boss. This scenario pales in comparison to malicious hackers removing speed warnings or railway signaling to cause deadly derailments of passenger trains.

If people are slow to update security patches and generally resist creating strong passwords, how can we expect to keep passengers and crew safe if we hand over control to hackers and their malware? As if railway operators don't already have enough on their shoulders, many are entrusted with the lives of hundreds of passengers on speeding trains. As we update and modernize all forms of railway equipment, we must also train the crews who operate them. That may not seem like a tall order until we take into account the staggering number of cyberbreaches due to negligence, ignorance, and laziness in the corporate workplace. In 2017, the total number of breached records exceeded two billion, and that was just data.[81] The increase in railway fatalities due to human error is usually rooted in distraction. Adding malicious terrorists and hackers into this mix only serves to raise these numbers.

CAR VULNERABILITIES

Cars have long played an integral role in the lives of so many, Americans in particular. Our US national highway system that began its build-out in the 1950s has blossomed into a sprawling and often construction zone–riddled network. The cars that populate these interconnected routes have evolved over the years to meet our consumer demands. Attributes like horsepower and torque have taken a backseat to features such as self-parking, entertainment centers, and Bluetooth connectivity. These days, teens approaching the legal driving age seem to be more interested in the freedom of the internet rather than cruising in a convertible Mustang. Most kids have the cash for a phone and a streaming music account but not for a new ride, so carmakers continue to focus on their parents,

---

81   Gemalto, "2017 Data Breach Level Index: Full Year Results Are In . . ." Gemalto, May 13, 2018, https://blog.gemalto.com/security/2018/04/13/data-breach-stats-for-2017-full-year-results-are-in/.

families, and upwardly mobile professionals of all types, and they want style too. The modern automobile has become the intersection where the digital and mechanical ages truly meet.

I mentioned the vast US highway system before because it serves as the backbone for the 268 million registered vehicles currently in operation. Over four million miles of roadways and 168,000 fueling stations ensure transportation of people and packages on a massive scale. One could easily liken our highway system to the internet, the cars to our mobile devices, and passengers to our data. By now, I think you know where I'm going with this analogy, but I believe there are some valid comparisons.

After the first car I owned, the cherry-red Mazda RX-7, was stolen but retrieved by the police, I decided to upgrade the alarm system, install a removable CD player, and utilize the Club steering wheel lock wherever I parked. Now that I've completely dated myself and confused my millennial readers, I can explain my safeguards only as a necessary step to ensure the safety of my investment. Remember, the average car price then and now constitutes a giant portion of most annual wages. Put it another way: What's the first thing you shop for after purchasing your brand new $1,000 iPhone X? Assuming you already have some kind of insurance, you probably opt for a protective case. After that, you setup your PIN—and if you require only four digits to unlock your phone, stop reading and upgrade to a six-digit PIN minimum right now. Then you probably log in to your iCloud or similar smartphone location service. These precautions have become second nature to any experienced mobile phone user because they value their investment. What happens when the $32,169 car (the current average cost of a new vehicle) you just bought is as vulnerable to hacking and theft as your smartphone? We're not just talking about a lot of money; we're talking about your safety and that of your passengers and anyone else on the road.

You might not remember their names, but you have probably heard about the Jeep Cherokee that was hacked a few years back in the summer of 2015. Charlie Miller and Chris Valasek were the two researchers who sent shock waves through Detroit and the cybersecurity research community simultaneously. By sending messages directly from their off-the-shelf laptop to their automobile's Controlled Area Network (CAN), they caused the vehicle to perform actions beyond the driver's control. These hacks included control over the air conditioning, GPS, stereo, transmission, and even the vehicle's braking system. Their first attacks were more physical in nature because it required a direct connection to the vehicle's CAN, but that all changed soon thereafter. The car-hacking duo next released partial code they'd developed to remotely hack any Chrysler vehicle that used the UConnect wireless standard, which meant that millions of vehicles and their drivers were vulnerable to remote hackers. Fortunately, Charlie and Chris are white hats and only wanted to point out those vulnerabilities to automakers and other hackers so that other cars and their CANs can be secured.

If you have purchased an automobile in the past few years, your car already has integrated cellular modems (likely 4G LTE) that communicate wirelessly through the cellular wide area network (WAN), the same networks that our smartphones use. Carmakers love the ability to push notifications and updates directly to our dashboards because that can deliver software as a direct service to millions of vehicles instantly without the need to schedule appointments and occupy valuable space in dealer garages. But like any electronic convenience, that one also opens the door to hackers and exploits, and there is no sign of slowing down from either side.

Modern automobiles continue to pack in technology and features, including advanced driver assistance systems (ADAS), instrument clusters, rear-parking camera assist, and the infotainment system. Just like any operating system, as these systems continue to grow, so do their attack vectors. Bluetooth, Wi-Fi, and cellular connectivity allow ease of access into any vehicle's engine control unit (ECU) from anywhere in the world. So the cat and mouse game that security experts and hackers play has literally taken to the streets, but are carmakers ready to take on the fight?

The National Highway Traffic Safety Administration (NHTSA) revealed that 738 people died in 2017 due to tire-related crashes, and since tire pressure is the most important part of tire maintenance, the US automotive industry has mandated that all vehicles made after 2008 must be equipped with tire-pressure monitoring systems (TPMS).[82] TPMS is an electronic system that monitors tire

---

82   National Highway Traffic Safety Administration, "Tire Maintenance Safety Tips," updated May 7, 2019, https://www.nhtsa.gov/equipment/tires.

air pressure and automatically transmits warning signals to the driver in the event of an overinflated or underinflated tire. However, automobile manufacturers cannot agree on a single standard. The majority of systems use direct tire sensors that transmit real-time tire pressure information to the vehicle's dashboard. The actual sensors are physical pressure transducers attached directly to the back of the valve stem or branded to the physical wheel. This means that the TPMS data cannot be hardwired.

All TPMS sensors—and anything that transmits an RF signal—must be approved by the Federal Communications Commission (FCC) to ensure no interference with other RF signals. Most direct TPMS use ultrahigh frequency (UHF) radio, which is typically 434 MHz, while many aftermarket TPMS systems utilize Bluetooth at 2.4 GHz. Neither of those standards contain built-in security, which leaves them open to nearby hackers. And since auto manufacturers cannot agree on a single TPMS standard, they are left to pursue the one that best fits their different business models and existing infrastructures. This lack of regulation and standards consolidation can foster healthy competition but also leads to marketplace confusion and safety standards reliant on a technology with little to no future. And this is just tire pressure, one example of technology making its way into our cars.

If it sounds like our cars are increasingly resembling our computers and smartphones, then you have been paying attention. Today's iOS vulnerabilities will resemble tomorrow's BMW vulnerabilities. No one is expecting perfect security for our computers in any industry, but can we really take that chance on the roads?

PROTECTING YOUR CARS

The recommended steps for protecting your truck, fleet vehicles, company car, and of course, your own pride and joy are all similar and will sound familiar to any security-minded computer user. To ensure a safe and stable vehicle, car owners need to maintain the latest firmware updates. All modern vehicles include USB ports, so it's important that vehicle owners never connect any unknown devices to them or install any unauthorized software through them. Most hacks still require physical access to a vehicle, so owners should inspect automobiles for any kind of tampering or hire an authorized mechanic to do it for them. When inserted into a vehicle's infotainment console, even a seemingly harmless USB stick can seriously compromise security and infect vehicle diagnostics and controls.

Since 1996, all US vehicles have been required to include an Onboard Diagnostic System II (OBD-II) port to be physically compliant. OBD-II is a self-diagnostic and reporting system that gives the vehicle owner or repair technician access to the status of the various vehicle subsystems. This requirement also means that the OBD-II connector, which is usually located under the steering column, on all vehicles could be used for a malware attack. Physical security is important for more than just protecting valuables inside the vehicle itself now, so lock your vehicle at all times and note any suspicious vehicle behavior, especially after having a car serviced.

In 2016, the FBI and NHTSA issued a warning to all drivers that motor vehicles are "increasingly vulnerable" to cyberattacks.[83] The warning came on the heels of massive recalls and security updates from major manufacturers. Remember the Chrysler Jeep that was hacked? It seems that the efforts of Charlie Miller and Chris Valasek did not go unnoticed. In July 2015—only one month after that Jeep was hacked—Chrysler recalled roughly 1.4 million vehicles for security patches that could not be administered digitally, and in 2017, two senators introduced the Spy Car Act. This legislation would direct the government to create standards to protect cars and their drivers from hacks.

When I appeared on i24 News from its New York studio in January 2019, I boldly claimed that no security-minded person should buy a new car.[84] I wasn't referring to any new vehicle safety or antitheft features, nor was I trying to make headlines, although I did get some strange looks. I stand behind my proclamation due to the lack of cybersecurity standards and ease of interconnectivity between all of the components found in the latest automobiles. Older vehicles use miles of cabling and physical switches to connect the driver and passengers to cars' luxury features; there were no wireless media entertainment centers that also connected back to the vehicle's ECU just a few years ago. The modern connectivity surely has its conveniences, but convenience typically supplants security. That is why, if you must replace your

---

83   Mark Rockwell, "FBI, NHTSA Issue Warning on Vehicle Hacks," FCW.com, March 18, 2016, https://fcw.com/articles/2016/03/18/car-hacking.aspx.

84   i24News, "This Is Why You Should Not Buy a New Car This Year," i24News, January 11, 2019, https://youtu.be/MVcceKc7L5k.

old ride and you're as cybersecurity obsessed as I am, I recommend buying a nice used car or last year's model without all of the wireless bells and whistles.

We have set a course for innovation and efficiency in our vehicles, so there is no turning back. Cars will continue to become even more personalized. The cars of the future will know who we are when entering the vehicle, and they will entertain us while we drive based on our preferences and personalities. Even people who don't own cars will still maintain relationships with this technology. Autonomous cars will soon flood the streets and get us to our destinations, and they will be just as vulnerable as any other modern taxi or owner-operator vehicle. There will be real and attempted hacks of different kinds to all cars, but the automakers building the most secure platforms will be rewarded with customers who appreciate secure transportation. Brand value of automobiles will be determined by safety and privacy standards rather than just speed and flashy tailfins. So whether you are a passenger or a driver, you are a direct participant in your own safety on the literal "information superhighway."

 POP QUIZ:
Which part of your car is the most vulnerable to hacking?

A. Cruise control.

B. Entertainment system.

C. Wireless key fob.

CHAPTER 23

Skimming from the Digital Till

Very few businesses are strictly cash these days. If you run a business or have ever worked in the service or retail industry, you probably have some experience with credit cards and point-of-sale (POS) systems. And just because most businesses accept credit cards does not mean that they also don't accept cash, so you must have some experience with ATMs and cash too. A skimmer is a hidden attachable device that records and stores every ATM or retail transaction at a given spot; it's a criminal's dream and every consumer's nightmare. You might have heard of this term and know a little about credit-fraud scams, but do you know when the first known skimming device was discovered?

Back in 2002, *CBS News* reported on the first known ATM skimmer found in the wild; until then, it was only a myth. But by 2003, the skimmer became an ugly truth when one New York City deli ATM had over $200,000 of theft in a single day. Law enforcement began to take notice, and the number of skimmers discovered since then has risen dramatically; the installation methods and locales of these illegal devices suggest that skimmer thieves have become much more brazen. If you think national bank chains are immune to skimmers, think again. If you think your local gas station where you fill up your tank every week is skimmer free, don't be so sure. And if you think your employees couldn't manage to steal from your customers electronically, you might want to look a little closer.

SKIMMER DATA

ATM skimmer theft alone has reached $2 billion per year globally with new law enforcement task forces being formed regularly to discover, dissect, and bust these elaborate criminal schemes.[85] Skimming devices have evolved from early mechanical scams that physically trapped a consumer's debit card, to malware that could infect a network of ATMs and forcing them to spit out wads

---

85   Jennifer Schlesinger and Andrea Day, "Card Sharks: ATM Skimming Grows More Sophisticated," CNBC, September 16, 2017, https://www.cnbc.com/2017/09/15/card-sharks-atm-skimming-grows-more-sophisticated.html.

of cash, to every iteration in between. The intersection of old-school robbers and high-tech hackers falls precisely at highly trafficked areas where consumers need cash and want to make quick purchases. This cashless theft involves data that is then sold on the Dark Web to other hackers and the highest bidders, but as we know, the damage continues even after the fraudulent purchases are credited back to the victims' accounts. Skimmer data plays a vital role in identity theft and the overall weakening of cybersecurity for billions of consumers.

One of the most ingenious skimming devices involves a simple magnetic head that reads unsuspecting users' cards as they are swiped. Since the skimmer is either placed on top of the existing POS swiper or lines the inside of a legitimate card swiper, it does not affect the user's experience at all. In fact, the users are the physical perpetrators *and* victims of the crime by swiping their own cards. Consumers still get their cash or pay for their goods/services, and the criminals get a copy of their account name, card number, expiration date, and security code all from a quick swipe. Pinhole cameras are also placed near keypads to capture PIN entry. Once the criminals have access to your credit or debit card data and your PIN, creating multiple copies of your card is a trivial matter. In order to retrieve that data, thieves used to physically connect to the skimmer to download it, but the wireless age has new conveniences for everyone, including criminals.

SERVICE STATIONS' RISKS

These days, criminals prefer to sit in their cars and wirelessly download the data with Bluetooth skimmers.

These skimmers leverage the ubiquity of low-cost Bluetooth transceivers and are usually found in gas pumps because service station fuel pumps are notoriously easy to open and tamper with. Some of these skimmers tap into the gas pump's power source for continuous operation, while others use batteries that eventually die. In either case, authorities usually discover the skimmers but not before checking hundreds or even thousands of nearby gas pumps. When a slew of credit-fraud reports begins to manifest in one region, task force agents must triangulate all of those accounts to locate the hidden skimmer(s). With roughly 150,000 gas stations in the US, there simply isn't enough time or manpower to continually search for hidden skimmers inside every gas pump. This Whac-A-Mole game played by law enforcement is time sensitive and got me thinking about a tool that could help alleviate the problem that agents face. After all, I know about wireless product design and have relationships with thousands of law enforcement customers.

Before one can fight crime, one must better understand the nature of that crime and its perpetrator. In late 2017, I presented at a security conference in Florida; its location was not a coincidence. The area was an apparent hotbed of skimmer activity and the target of a Russian skimming ring run out of central Florida, except these skimmers were found hidden inside hundreds of gas pumps located directly off the interstate highway. I was to present technical details and possible solutions for detecting wireless skimmers, but just before my presentation, a senior law enforcement agent in the middle of an undercover sting operation supplied the attendees with a fascinating glimpse into his work. Arthur (not his real name) delivered a compelling account of his investigation and supplied my engineering team and me with valuable insights into the criminal mind and preferred methods of attack.

INSIDE A SKIMMING INVESTIGATION

With its high-end restaurants and wealthy socialite patrons, the southwest coast of Florida has become a major target for credit fraud. The investigation began when Arthur's department received an anonymous tip about the credit cards of wealthy individuals being stolen, or more accurately, used in committing identity theft crimes. For US banks, credit fraud is as common as interest payments. This is partly due to the fact that US security standards lag behind the rest of the world and partly because US banks go out of their way to accommodate customers defrauded by identity theft. Rather than working with law enforcement to prevent fraudulent activity, the banks simply absorb the fraud costs and raise interest rates for all of their customers. This is just another in an infinitely long list of examples where security takes a backseat to convenience and revenue generators are disguised as cost-saving measures.

As the investigation unfolded, Arthur began to interview numerous customers complaining that their credit cards were compromised shortly after dining at a particular restaurant. Arthur met with the owner to review the books, and while the owner was fairly certain that one of the employees might be behind the thievery, they were not sure where to begin. Since it was, apparently, an inside job that involved many thousands of dollars being stolen over a period of time, Arthur decided to inject himself into the restaurant's daily operation so he could flush out the thief. After performing a thorough background check on every employee, everything seemed ordinary. The owner happened to be looking for a dishwasher at the time, so Arthur decided that would be the perfect opportunity to go undercover. He put in the long hours washing dishes, slowly blending in and earning the staff's trust. For days, Arthur closely watched the register and staff, but nothing looked suspicious. As the weeks continued to pass, still nothing aroused his suspicion until one day a waitress arrived at the restaurant in a brand new, top-of-the-line Cadillac. The $80,000 sticker price for a vehicle owned by a waitress, who was mostly getting by on her tips, was more than enough to finally stoke Arthur's suspicions.

With an eagle eye watching her every move, Arthur was able to spot the crime as it happened, but just barely. When it came time to process a payment, the wily waitress would disappear around the corner and out of view from the entire restaurant staff and customers. While gone only for an instant, she would casually lower her hand holding the credit card and just like that, the card was skimmed by a device buried in her apron. It all happened so fast that Arthur had to view it repeatedly to see the pattern and catch the moment of skimming. The crime was very well choreographed, much like a skilled magician working on stage in front of everyone. We see only what the magician wants us to see.

In this instance, a corrupt employee was manually using a simple swiper device to record card data, but many skimmers work 24-7 when integrated within all-day service station pumps and/or ATMs. If I were to aid law enforcement, these would be my primary targets because they account for so much fraudulent activity.

BLUETOOTH A TARGET

According to the Bluetooth Special Interest Group (SIG), over four billion Bluetooth devices were shipped in 2018 alone.[86] When added to the billions of Bluetooth devices already in use since 1998, they now easily outnumber all of the people on the planet. With so many wireless signals bouncing around our public spaces, it can be extremely difficult to identify the malicious ones from the friendly ones. But by crafting a directional antenna attuned to Bluetooth's RF signature, along with simple software that identifies known malicious Bluetooth devices, law enforcement still has a fighting chance.

When I visited that security conference in Florida, I brought with me a prototype tool to aid law enforcement agents in the field. Federal agents from the US Weights and Measures Division have been working with local law enforcement over the past few years on the growing problem of skimmers found in gas pumps. I tailed along on one of those expeditions and brought a prototype receiver capable of detecting suspicious Bluetooth activity from

86   Brian Buntz, "Bluetooth SIG Exec on Why Bluetooth Mesh Is an IIoT Enabler," IoT World Today, September 25, 2018, https://www.iotworldtoday.com/2018/09/25/bluetooth-sig-exec-on-why-bluetooth-mesh-is-an-iiot-enabler/.

a distance. The technology is certainly nothing new; my company has been selling similar devices to agents tasked with securing all wireless data in federal facilities for over a decade now. But this particular device might change the equation for law enforcement trying to locate a skimmer needle in a Bluetooth haystack.

The agents immediately understood its measurements and potential, but after several more hours under the Florida sun, it was time to call it a day. The areas we searched that day were all known hotspots for hidden skimmers, but we didn't find any after opening up dozens of service station pumps. But this was actually a good thing because our Bluetooth skimmer detector didn't either, meaning no false positives. Until now, law enforcement had to rely solely on tips and suspicions before traveling to gas stations, filling out paperwork for impromptu inspections, and contacting gas station managers to accompany them in physically opening and inspecting each and every pump. Once inside a suspected pump with a hidden skimmer, a visual inspection can still take up to ten minutes each.

PROTECTION IDEAS

Consumer advocate groups offer many safety and security tips to help avoid skimmers and other criminal activity. One common suggestion for consumers worried about Bluetooth skimmers is to pull out your smartphone and check for suspicious Bluetooth devices by using either the phone's built-in scanned device list or a dedicated app. While this is well-meaning advice, it offers little value because smartphones lack the proper antenna configurations to detect, much less locate, any Bluetooth skimmers. A consumer standing right near a skimmer might see that skimmer's ID pop up on their scan list, but then what? How do they know the suspicious Bluetooth device ID is located in the pump they are facing, the one next to that, or the one ten feet away? All they can do is avoid that service station until they feel safe.

While consumers should report any suspicious skimmer activity to the station's manager or local authorities, they simply cannot identify the ever-changing device IDs appearing on their phones. Criminals are fully aware that smartphones can be used to potentially detect skimmer IDs, so they counter by changing and updating their Bluetooth chipsets to avoid detection. Consumers should always report suspicious criminal activity to the authorities, but the real detective work needs to be left to the professionals.

Having a wireless tool at their disposal can greatly increase the number of skimmers recovered every day and free up law enforcement to spend more time hunting down the perpetrators rather than just the artifacts of their criminal efforts. And speaking of hunting down, since Bluetooth detection requires a pairing of devices, there is a very good chance this technology will also lead to the detection and location of the nearby criminals as they download the data. I look forward to headlines reading, "Bluetooth Skimmer Criminals Caught Red-Handed."

An interesting side effect to our BVS Bluetooth skimmer detector comes in the form of our customers. While primarily law enforcement agents, part of our customer base now includes fuel delivery and dispensary service providers. These giant fuel truck drivers are being armed with more than just the keys. By using wireless security products to detect hidden skimmers, the fuel dispensaries are adding value to their services and increasing their own revenue streams. In this case, the service station, the fuel dispensary providers, and ultimately the customers all benefit from detecting and preventing fraud. Talk about cybersecurity being everybody's business!

BANK VULNERABILITIES

Skimmed card data generally takes a circuitous path from a semiorganized crime ring into the Dark Web, where that same card data is either cloned, sold to the highest bidder, or recompiled into lists of other cards that float around black markets for months on end. And after all of this, customers are still not alerted to any fraudulent activity until the charges begin appearing from stolen cards. If the customers do eventually notice unauthorized charges, they simply contact their bank, are issued a new card number, and the fraudulent charges are generally credited back to the customers' accounts.

Based on my conversations with major US banks, and contrary to their claims, they are *not* in the business of fraud prevention, and if you read my first book, I explain why banks are not high on my list of trusted businesses either. They prefer to turn a blind eye to the criminal world that manufactures, installs, and maintains skimmers inside thousands of their ATMs around the world.

Most skimmers inserted into ATMs are as thin as the cards they steal data from. This thinness isn't a bragging right like we see in the smartphone market, but rather a requirement, since it's the only way to install and conceal a skimmer. Unlike gas pumps, ATMs are guarding thousands of dollars and tend to incorporate thick steel doors with tamper-proof locking mechanisms. The banks effectively engineered the structural integrity of their ATMs to protect the cash but never really considered a digital theft straight through the debit card slot itself. With the aid of a homemade tool placed right down the neck of the card reader, thieves can quickly install a skimmer into most any ATM. If they have an accomplice or an insider, they can place that skimmer in less than thirty seconds. And because debit cards require a manually entered security PIN, tiny pinhole cameras usually accompany these covert installations to capture the digits when entered by the customer. So not only do you have to worry about the guy looking over your shoulder, you have to also worry about the camera streaming your PIN to the suspicious car parked nearby.

If you use your small business or consumer debit card at an ATM, there are several precautions you can take. Begin by using common sense and thoroughly scanning the area surrounding the ATM for anything suspicious, including a close inspection of the ATM itself. Ask yourself whether the ATM belongs in a dark alley or even on the sidewalk. Before inserting your card, physically check the machine for anything suspicious, such as loose plastic, misaligned plastic bezel housings around the card's insertion slot, or keypad alterations for any signs of tampering. If you have a keen eye, look for a tiny pinhole camera that is usually located within a few inches of the keypad. To be safe, use only ATMs in busy pedestrian areas, as these machines are much less likely to include hidden skimmers. And of course, always monitor your financial statements carefully for any strange activity.

As a security expert, I have always advocated for cash purchases when convenient, but it's getting more difficult to recommend cash when the ATMs themselves might be rigged to steal directly from consumers. The financial industry has also changed; more and more banks have attracted online customers and reduced their retail hours, making it challenging to obtain cash from a real person. As a result, I prefer services like Apple Pay, which uses near field communication (NFC) instead of the credit or debit card in my wallet. Android Pay, Samsung Pay, and Apple Pay are all far more secure than traditional card payments because they use end-to-end encryption and one-time tokenized transactions rather than holding, storing, and sending actual account information. This makes NFC hacking difficult, if not impossible.

In early 2018, reports emerged from law enforcement regarding card skimmers with cellular connectivity. This wireless connectivity is no different than any consumer cell phone, meaning that cyberthieves can hide a cellular skimmer inside any ATM and then access the card data it has stolen from anywhere in the world. But cellular skimmers like this require a SIM card to activate it for use on the global cellular network. This SIM card could serve as a bread-crumb trail back to the owner if they are not careful to remain anonymous. And just like with any phone, wireless carriers can shut off SIM connectivity if authorities suspect the account is being used for illegal purposes. As is always the case with cybercriminals, you must weigh the likelihood of them adopting new skimmer technology with the potential convenience of a given cellular device. I'm actually surprised we haven't seen more of these new cellular skimmers on the scene, given the typical hacker's "work ethic." Bluetooth skimmers won't be replaced by this new crop of cellular skimmers anytime soon, but the future of wireless skimming has arrived, and it promises to deliver more skimming fraud than ever.

SMART CARDS AND SHIMMERS

Meanwhile, the United States is now joining the rest of the world by requiring merchants to upgrade their POS terminals to support chip-enabled cards. Conventional magnetic stripe cards are notoriously easy to read and copy without involving any security authentication or encryption. Chip-and-PIN cards, also known as "smart cards," contain an integrated circuit that uses a PIN and cryptographic algorithms for improved data security over magnetic strips.

Smart cards have been in use for many years internationally but have begun to appear only recently in the United States. Unfortunately, before security experts could even breathe a collective sigh of relief, a new threat appeared. While magnetically striped cards can be compromised by skimmers, smart cards can be compromised by "shimmers." A leading expert on spam, skimming, and many other digital security issues, Brian Krebs first reported on these so-called shimmers back in August 2015. In his KrebsonSecurity.com blog from January 2018, Brian explains the difference between skimmers and shimmers:

"Most skimming devices made to steal credit card data do so by recording the data stored in plain text on the magnetic stripe on the backs of cards. A shimmer, on the other hand, is so named because it acts as a shim that sits between the chip on the card and the chip reader in the ATM or point-of-sale device—recording the data on the chip as it is read by the underlying machine."

Krebs goes on to describe shimmers as harder to spot because they are always located inside the compromised machines without the need for external skimmer artifices. This does limit the number of overall ATM targets, but chip-and-PIN cards have just begun to take hold in the United States, so the growth potential of smart cards is matched only by their hacking potential. Of course, even if these shimmers are discovered, all ATMs still use swiper mechanisms for the magnetic strip located on the back of all cards. This fifty-year-old magnetic stripe technology will continue to serve as the backup transaction method in millions of retail POS terminals and ATMs until the United States catches up with the rest of the developed nations.

I fear it will be quite some time before we begin to hear about any slowdown in skimmer/shimmer fraud, but until then, we can only work to protect our personal and business accounts from skimming threats. By following best practices and keeping an eye out for suspicious-looking POS terminals and corrupt retailers that operate them, consumers and business owners are the true prevention firewall standing between criminals and consumers.

 POP QUIZ:
Which one of these statements is false?

A. Tokenized transactions are more secure than credit cards.

B. Card skimmers can be hidden inside ATMs.

C. Bluetooth skimmers are detected by using smartphones.

CHAPTER 24

In Big Data We Do Not Trust

2018 will go down as the year that big data went down too. No, Google wasn't breached by Anonymous who proceeded to spill all of our private search queries into the streets, but something just as bad for Google did happen. Facebook, Amazon, Google—the three biggest US data collectors—and even Apple all lost the public trust in varying degrees.

AMAZON

Amazon played a game with New York City—and every other city believing it had a chance—in order to receive a reported $3 billion in tax credits for building its new headquarters (HQ2) in Queens, New York, and Amazon lost. When Queens residents protested HQ2, Amazon "just took their ball and went home," according to a furious Mayor Bill de Blasio, giving no counterproposal or explanation.[87]

On top of the HQ2 debacle, Amazon become embroiled in a facial-recognition technology brouhaha that pitted its investors against its bottom line. An activist investor group demanded that Amazon halt sales of the facial-recognition systems to government agencies over fear that the technology would be used to violate people's rights.[88] Amazon has yet to react or even offer an explanation for its future plans involving the technology, but as a result, the friendly Alexa voice assistant has lost some of its luster.

GOOGLE

Google was slapped with a record-breaking antitrust fine of $5 billion by the EU. We've seen this before. Back in the 1990s, Microsoft was hit with an antitrust fine over bundling its browser and operating system together. Apparently,

---

87   Jake Kanter, "Amazon Investors Are Cranking Up the Pressure on Jeff Bezos to Stop Selling Facial Recognition Tech to Government Agencies," Business Insider, January 17, 2019, https://www.insider.com/amazon-shareholders-submit-resolution-on-halting-rekognition-sales-2019-1.

88   Nolan Hicks, "Furious de Blasio Says Amazon 'Disrespected' NYC by Ditching HQ2 Deal," New York Post, February 15, 2019, https://nypost.com/2019/02/15/furious-de-blasio-says-amazon-disrespected-nyc-by-ditching-hq2-deal/.

Google didn't take heed when it bundled its own search engine and Chrome apps under one Android operating system. Adding insult to antitrust, Google went on to allegedly make payments to "certain large manufacturers and mobile network operators," according to the European Commission, in order to exclusively bundle its search app onto handsets.[89]

Aside from the steep fine, Google was quietly working on controversial projects that were both shuttered once its own employees caught wind of them and threatened to quit. Project Maven was Google's attempt to work with the Pentagon in analyzing drone footage, but as you can imagine, these drones were not very consumer friendly. Another secret project involving a censored search engine developed just for China by Google left a bad taste in everyone's mouth once word got out that they planned to profit off the suppression of free information to 1.3 billion people. They pulled the plug on this venture, too, but it just goes to show you that the East and West not only have eyes on each other but also on each other's tech companies.

APPLE

Even though Apple isn't considered a big data company when compared to Google, it wasn't immune to the sting of doing business in China either. After receiving widespread criticism for opening its iCloud servers to Chinese authorities, both Apple and Amazon were accused

---

89   Tom Warren, "Google Fined a Record $5 Billion they the EU for Android Antitrust Violations," The Verge, July 18, 2018, https://www.theverge.com/2018/7/18/17580694/google-android-eu-fine-antitrust.

of using motherboards containing spy chips from China and then lying about it. However, after lengthy inspections and hardware audits, no proof has ever surfaced; their accusers at *Bloomberg* have never issued an apology or retraction, so the mystery looms.

Apple tried to fight its way back into the hearts of privacy-minded folks by stealing the spotlight during the 2019 Consumer Electronics Show (CES) in Las Vegas when a giant iPhone ad was plastered across a skyscraper: "What happens on your iPhone stays on your iPhone." Unfortunately, a few days later, a nasty bug surfaced allowing anyone using FaceTime groups to spy on the other people in that group before a call was even connected. Also, that skyscraper I mentioned . . . it was actually a Marriot hotel. If you're not already laughing and you enjoy irony, I highly recommend you reread the Marriot breach chapter.

FACEBOOK
Of all the big-data and tech companies, Facebook stands out as the one that lost the most public trust, and yet its stock price is still strong. Why? Part of Facebook's appeal to investors is the same one that defines the relationship between drug dealers and their customers. Facebook users have full control over their faculties, and I haven't heard of any fatal Facebook overdoses; yet Facebook users all begrudgingly tell me that they are addicted to the service. Facebook squandered its monopoly social media lead by converting nearly two billion loyal, happy users into distrustful and reluctant customers. Many have left the service due to the poor privacy policies, while others

left as a result of trolls and bullying that turned some "friends" into enemies.

The first few months of 2018 were among the worst for Facebook, but the rest of the year never really got much better. After testifying before Congress for five hours straight over election-integrity issues and data misuse, Mark Zuckerberg tried to put the entire Cambridge Analytica data scandal[90] behind him, but that was just the beginning. With "Fake news" on the lips of the president at every turn and news media trying to improve their trust with the American people, Facebook found itself in the middle of this battle.

Sometimes Facebook would pull down controversial pages after urging from users and watchdog groups against hate speech, and other times Facebook would fight those requests. Its editorial oversight department sent a confused message that Facebook was both a social media company and a content media company at the same time.

In July 2018, Facebook finally relented and suspended InfoWars and Alex Jones for promoting fake news. They followed that up by shutting down four of Jones's Facebook pages for hate-speech violations, but it was too late. At that point, users weren't just confused about Facebook speech policies—they became confused about what Facebook stood for. Is the proud mother sharing her family photos really supposed to ingest a diet of hate and fake news just to pad Facebook's ad revenue bottom line? I would normally tell any unhappy customer to leave Facebook for a competing

---

90   Nicholas Confessore, "Cambridge Analytica and Facebook: The Scandal and the Fallout So Far," *New York Times*, April 4, 2018, https://www.nytimes.com/2018/04/04/us/politics/cambridge-analytica-scandal-fallout.html.

service, but there is no competition unless you consider Instagram, which is owned by Facebook, as an alternative.

After hours of testimony before Congress, even Mark Zuckerberg had to admit that Facebook has a veritable monopoly on social media. But we cannot simply ascribe pure greed to Facebook's poor user and public trust status.

Facebook advertisers' single goal is to get as many clicks as possible for their money. I have no problem with advertising in general, but when you create a platform like Facebook that strives only for user engagement, you are not putting user interests above other interests—and that includes your advertisers. We all know how this plays out. If you click on a video about vegetarianism, you will next be fed (no pun intended) a series of vegan videos, followed by raw-vegan videos, followed by fasting videos, and so on. Facebook and the internet community as a whole know that extremism is rewarded by user engagement in the form of comments, dislikes, and shares. This finds its way into all forms of social media.

For example, back in 2016, I was invited to demonstrate some contraband detection products for the local *NBC News* I-Team to use in a piece they were developing around a surge of contraband phones smuggling into Rikers Island prison. After the interview aired, BVS posted the clip on our YouTube channel and received several thousand views and a handful of comments. In 2017, Mayor Bill de Blasio announced his intent to close Rikers Island, and since then, the same video has received over 175,000 views, close to 1,000 likes, and hundreds of comments. This was great news for my company since we were indirectly advertising our products for correctional facilities, but not so great for the guards, staff, and politicians due to the racially motivated hate found in most of the comments. Algorithms simply don't care about user feelings or even facts. These systems are in place only to generate user engagement, and user engagement is in place only to serve advertising dollars. After all, Facebook's real customers are its advertisers; its users are "the product."

THE UPSHOT

"You are our customer. You are a jewel, and we care," said Apple CEO Tim Cook in a recent interview on April 6, 2018, with MSNBC's Chris Hayes when he was asked about user privacy. I cannot imagine Mark Zuckerberg even attempting to mouth those words, but that didn't stop him from criticizing Cook's remarks as "extremely glib." Meanwhile, Facebook still refuses to categorize itself as a media entity, even though it produces and distributes more content than any other media company in the world. Facebook continues to apologize each time the algorithms fail to correctly identify hate speech or fake news ads, and yet the entire company is based on AI and advanced algorithms to accurately populate users' feeds. This chapter wasn't intended to be a Facebook hit piece, but it might seem that way, so I'll change the subject to Google.

Google has been making some important gestures for the protection of user data in recent months, which is about time. When the EU's GDPR implementation deadline went into effect on May 28, 2018, Google stepped up its game in an effort to comply—not just with regulators but also with their customers' wishes for more transparency and control over their own data. Since Google is essentially still an advertising company, it has addressed privacy concerns using some of the GDPR designations, such as controller, processor, and co-controller. These designations are too complex to go into all the details here, but essentially, it means that Google will act as any three of these functions in order to maintain control over how data is processed and share the accountability with its publishers.

Unlike Facebook, Google is proactively taking self-regulation seriously. That does not always lead to the best outcome, but it shows that Google is listening to its critics and attempting to pivot. Another big step in that direction comes from Google's rejuvenated hardware push. By all accounts, Pixel 2 is not only a well-reviewed smartphone but also a major step in the right direction toward data privacy and security. The Pixel 2 and 2 XL models are the first to introduce a tamper-resistant security module to any smartphone running an Android OS. When coupled with Pixel's frequent security updates, this creates enterprise-grade security for any non-Apple smartphone. Unfortunately, Android continues to flounder over security issues. When a German security firm recently looked under the hood, it found that hundreds of different third-party devices running an Android OS not only failed to implement security patches but also misinformed users about the status of those patches.[91] Weak security

---

91   Andy Greenberg, "How Android Phones Hide Missed Security Updates From You," *Wired*, April 12, 2018, https://www.wired.com/story/android-phones-hide-missed-security-updates-from-you/.

is endemic for most third-party Android devices because device makers continually fail to offer timely security updates when Google issues them.

The other big players—Apple, Microsoft, and Amazon —subscribe to a slightly or wildly different business model, depending on the approach. There seems to be a distinct correlation between the reliance on revenue from hardware sales and a company's collection and treatment of its customers' data. And this treatment can greatly affect the public's trust. Apple is known for engendering massive customer loyalty and trust. The company makes its own proprietary hardware and software and still receives most of its revenue from hardware sales directly to the consumer. This gives Apple not only the most control over the customer experience but also the most control over that hardware's security. It also means that Apple doesn't have to scrape user data for advertising and marketing purposes. Apple knows exactly how its customers use their devices and does not need any data aggregators or advertisers in the mix. This might offer little comfort to privacy advocates, but when you consider Facebook's lax data security and sharing standards (i.e., Cambridge Analytica), Apple is in a completely different league than Facebook in terms of how many hands are on your data.

Or to put it another way, the expense to Apple customers is up front. For a steep price, you get luxury tech products all contained in a walled-garden ecosphere, including free security and feature patches. Full disclosure, I am an Apple fan and buy most of their products for that reason; I've also convinced my family members to buy into the Apple ecosystem.

With every other tech giant, you pay less up front but end up paying more and/or incur more risk later on. Microsoft has introduced a sleek line of laptop/tablet hybrids and stylish desktops that rival Apple's iMac, but they still run Windows. Microsoft also makes the bulk of its revenue from desktop OS and Office software sales, but it has made aggressive moves in big data by acquiring LinkedIn and, more recently, GitHub, a platform for software-developer collaboration. The Microsoft hardware lineup is promising but still nascent, so it continues to rely on malware-plagued Windows and software subscription models primarily running on third-party hardware—a challenging environment for Microsoft. As the provider for more laptop, desktop, and enterprise software than any company in the world, it needs to maintain customer trust; when cybercriminals prefer to target Microsoft over Adobe and Android, these are not the kind of supporters you want backing your platform.

Amazon is on track to surpass everyone in terms of overall valuation in the very near future. It just announced over one hundred million Prime subscribers and one hundred million Echo smart speaker devices sold, and they even have a growing brick-and-mortar presence. In fact, according to The Verge and Reticle Research, Amazon is trusted over all the major tech companies and just below your bank.[92] So how does this happen when Amazon is known

92   Nick Statt, "Amazon Is the Ruthless Corporate Juggernaut People Love," The Verge, October 27, 2017, https://www.theverge.com/2017/10/27/16552614/amazon-popularity-user-survey-prime-echo-trust.

worldwide for its predatory pricing? I think it comes back to the core business of convenience retail. Since Amazon sells so many physical items to so many customers, it's become the de facto online retailer for most. The same-day or two-day delivery promise contributes to customer trust, but very little is known about Amazon's massive data collection efforts. Amazon keeps specific sales numbers of Fire TV and Kindles to itself and are even cagier when it comes to user data.

Meanwhile, Amazon's lesser-known business of server cloud infrastructure is the company's real bread and butter. Amazon Web Services (AWS) holds about 33 percent of all cloud infrastructure. Netflix, Hulu, HBO, and pretty much any streaming video service you can think of rely on AWS. Microsoft is second with about 13 percent market share, and Google clocks in at only 6 percent. They are the three biggest players in both consumer-facing and behind-the-scenes big data.

As an Amazon Prime subscriber, I clearly see the value of its online shopping and streaming services, but I do not confuse that with Amazon's fixation of placing cameras inside most of its products, including alarm clocks, smart speakers, and fashion-tip technology. Like Google, the data Amazon scrapes off my account seems to follow me around the internet, but also like Facebook, the data Amazon gleans from me seems to only direct me back to Amazon itself, which is a smart business practice but annoying as a consumer being steered to a single platform. Amazon acts as both an open internet entity and a closed online store in which members get preferred treatment.

This raises all kinds of concerns that we are now just beginning to wade through with Facebook.

Of course, there are many more big players that I have not covered here, including Instagram and WhatsApp, which are both owned by Facebook; Twitter; and a slew of Asian tech companies like Alibaba, Tencent, and Baidu. China's AI data advancements are growing faster than ours, but US tech companies are still ahead in most areas for now. If nothing else comes from Facebook's recent fiascos, at least there is still a chance that regular users will come to understand the value of their data. Until that happens, however, no government regulation or self-regulation can truly help users decide which company to place their trust in.

 ## POP QUIZ:
Which one of these things is most effective for maintaining your digital privacy?

A. Unsubscribing from all spam emails.

B. Covering your computer's front-facing camera.

C. Not sharing personal information on social media.

Conclusion

There are many experts and colleagues I would like to thank for helping me make this book possible, but I will thank them in person and instead turn my attention to the readers. I want to thank you for investing your time and allowing me to share my story. I am grateful for your attention and all of the valuable feedback I have received since releasing *Hacked Again*. Please share any useful knowledge you feel you have gained from this book with your business colleagues, families, and friends. No one is 100 percent safe from cybercriminals, nor can we ever beat them individually. However, by collectively learning and sharing information, we will all stand a fighting chance to take control of our cybersecurity.

I have compared cybersecurity to a jigsaw puzzle to be completed by both sides of this fight for our privacy. Criminals piece together fragments of our hacked private information in order to form a full puzzle of our digital identities, but each piece of the cybersecurity puzzle *we* collect by learning how to protect ourselves can also effectively protect others. Some of us work the corners while others prefer to focus on visual cues or just use instinct, but when we all work together on the same puzzle, everyone benefits.

There are no shortcuts, CliffsNotes, or silver bullets to solving this puzzle. As small business owners and consumers, it takes time, energy, and effort, so let's all collectively roll up our sleeves to get the job done. After all, Cybersecurity Is Everybody's Business!

Stay Safe.

Pop Quiz

Chapter 1. The "Cyber" in Cybersecurity
What is the simplest way to stop brute-force cyberattacks dead in their tracks?

    A. Shred all paperwork containing sensitive information.

    B. Add a deadbolt lock to all entryways.

    C. Add a few unique characters to any password or PIN.

Chapter 2. Spies Like OS
What's the quickest way to stop a suspected app, device, or OS from spying on you?

    A. Google user reports of that device's spying activity and what those people did to stop it.

    B. Log out of the suspected device or account and go about your day.

    C. Visit Consumer Affairs or the Federal Trade Commission website for tips.

Chapter 3. Engineered for Social
What is the weakest link in cybersecurity?

    A. Weak encryption.

    B. Humans.

    C. Short passwords.

Chapter 4. Minding the Hack
What is the first thing you should do if your company is facing ransomware demands:

    A. Determine whether ransomware demand is legitimate and follow instructions to get your data back.

    B. Ignore the demands, but back up all data just in case.

    C. Contact police and do not pay the ransom.

Chapter 5. You're in Good Hands with Cyber Insurance
Which one of these things will a comprehensive cyber insurance NOT protect you from?

    A. Poor cybersecurity hygiene and implementation.

    B. A ransomware attack on your company's computer network.

    C. An employee skimming/stealing customers' credit cards.

Chapter 6. Do Not Read This Chapter until You've Done Just One Small Thing
What's the best way to secure a weak password like "monkey123"?

    A. Add an uppercase numeral and a special character, such as $.

    B. Don't reuse it anywhere else or share it with anyone.

    C. Enable two-factor authentication.

Chapter 7. Virtual Peace of Mind
When using a VPN, what's the one thing you cannot hide from ISPs, hackers, and the government?

    A. The fact that you're using a VPN.

    B. Your identity.

    C. Your data.

Chapter 8. Minimize Your Digital Footprints
The best way to minimize your digital footprint is to:

    A. Take fewer photos with your smartphone.

    B. Travel less with your smartphone.

    C. Post less on social media.

Chapter 9. Digital Spring Cleaning
What is most valuable to companies looking to sell you something?

    A. Your phone number.

    B. Your email address.

    C. Your physical address.

Chapter 10. Robocalls Have Gone Viral
What's the best way to deal with pesky robocalls?

    A. Ask to speak with their supervisor.

    B. Use a carrier-approved smartphone app.

    C. Register your phone number on the National Do Not Call Registry.

Chapter 11. Ashley Madison Is Cheating the Cheaters
Which organization is the most vulnerable to hacking?

    A. Charitable organizations with weak cybersecurity.

    B. Black market websites with strong cybersecurity.

    C. Your business.

Chapter 12. Yahoo Has Been Hacked Again and Again
When is it OK to reuse a password?

    A. When you are logging into social media accounts.

    B. When it is too hard to remember a long password.

    C. Never.

Chapter 13. Massive Breach Befitting a Massive Hotel Chain
What should you do if you think your identity or accounts have been compromised?

    A. Monitor your email address and accounts for fraudulent activity.

    B. Respond to the warning email you have received.

    C. Subscribe to a monitoring service such as Lifelock or WebWatcher.

Chapter 14. Opening a Can of Cyber Worms
The best defense against ransomware is being proactive when you:

    A. Purchase comprehensive cybersecurity insurance.

    B. Back up your data regularly.

    C. Regularly update all your devices and software with the latest security patches.

Chapter 15. The Internet of Stings
What's the best way to steer clear of IoT device security hacks?

A. Choose only name-brand hardware makers.

B. Disconnect IoT devices from the internet when you are not using them.

C. Do not purchase any IoT devices you do not need.

Chapter 16. Equifax and What Not to Do When You Are Hacked
What will freezing your credit not affect?

A. Vulnerability to identity theft.

B. Your credit score.

C. You need to monitor financial statements for fraud.

Chapter 17. Uber's Bumpy Ride
Which ridesharing service collects the least amount of your data?

A. Uber.

B. Lyft.

C. Public taxi service.

Chapter 18. Anthem's Unhealthy Breach
What is the best way to keep employees from falling for phishing scams?

    A. Email filters that block suspicious attachments.

    B. Cybersecurity awareness training.

    C. Pop-up blockers.

Chapter 19. The Battle over Our Data Has Just Begun
What is the best way to maintain privacy between two parties?

    A. Long and strong passwords and two-factor authentication.

    B. Encrypted cloud services.

    C. End-to-end encryption.

Chapter 20. Crypto Capitalism
Which of the following cryptocurrency statements is false:

    A. Blockchain is the digital ledger that records all cryptocurrency transactions.

    B. Each new Bitcoin mined requires slightly more energy than the previous one.

    C. Cryptocurrency is one hundred times more secure than traditional currency.

Chapter 21. Airborne Threats
If you see a suspicious or dangerous drone flying near you, you should:

    A. Call the police.

    B. Shoot it out of the sky.

    C. Call the FAA.

Chapter 22. Hacking Planes, Trains, and Automobiles
Which part of your car is the most vulnerable to hacking?

    A. Cruise control.

    B. Entertainment system.

    C. Wireless key fob.

Chapter 23. Skimming from the Digital Till
Which one of these statements is false?

    A. Tokenized transactions are more secure than credit cards.

    B. Card skimmers can be hidden inside ATMs.

    C. Bluetooth skimmers are detected by using smartphones.

Chapter 24. In Big Data We Do Not Trust
Which one of these things is most effective for maintaining your digital privacy?

    A. Unsubscribing from all spam emails.

    B. Covering your computer's front-facing camera.

    C. Not sharing personal information on social media.

Pop Quiz Answers:

1.   C
2.   B
3.   B
4.   C
5.   A
6.   C (But you should also immediately change your password.)
7.   A
8.   C
9.   A
10.   B
11.   A (And, hopefully, not your business)
12.   C
13.   A
14.   B
15.   C
16.   B
17.   C
18.   B
19.   C
20.   C
21.   A
22.   B
23.   C
24.   C

Glossary of Cybersecurity Terms

I am providing this rich glossary of cybersecurity terms that appeared in my first book, *Hacked Again*. I hope that long after you have read this book, you can refer back to any terms as a refresher.

Academy of Model Aeronautics (AMA): Academy of Model Aeronautics is a nonprofit organization dedicated to the promotion of model aviation as a recognized sport including recreational activity. www.modelaircraft.org

Access Point (AP): A device that allows wireless devices to connect to a wired network using Wi-Fi or related standards.

Advanced Driver Assistance Systems (ADAS): A system that aids the driver in the driving process. This human machine interface ultimately will improve the overall car and road safety.

Air Transport Action Group (ATAG): A well-respected non-profit group of industry experts that focus on issues of the air transport industry. www.atag.org

Anonymous: A group of hacktivist entities known for well-publicized publicity stunts and DDoS attacks against government, religious, and corporate websites.

Antivirus software: A program that monitors a computer or network to detect or identify major types of malicious code and to prevent or contain malware incidents, sometimes by removing or neutralizing the malicious code.

Artificial Intelligence (AI): Intelligence that is demonstrated by machines as opposed to intelligence that is naturally displayed by people. Often, AI machines or computers are mimicking the cognitive functions people exhibit, such as learning and problem-solving.

Attack: An attempt to gain unauthorized access to system services, resources, or information or an attempt to compromise system integrity.

Backdoor: In a computer system, a method of bypassing normal authentication and securing unauthorized remote access to a computer.

Bitcoin: A type of digital currency in which encryption techniques are used to regulate the generation of units of currency and verify the transfer of funds while operating independently of a central bank. Many Bitcoin transactions are associated with illegal Dark Web activity, but not all. Payment by Bitcoin allows cyberthieves to remain completely anonymous.

Black hat: A hacker who uses his or her abilities for malicious or selfish purposes.

Blacklist: A list of entities that are blocked or denied privileges or access.

Bluetooth: A wireless technology standard (IEEE 802.15) for exchanging data over relatively short distances. This standard was initially conceived as a wireless alternative to the popular RS-232 data cables.

Bot: One computer connected to the internet that has been surreptitiously/secretly compromised with malicious logic to perform activities under the command and control of a remote administrator.

Botnet: A collection of computers compromised by malicious code and controlled across a network.

Brute-force attack: This type of computer attack aims at being the simplest kind of method to gain access to a site: it tries usernames and passwords over and over again until it gets in.

Bulletin Board Systems (BBS): A computer server running software that allows users to connect to the system using a terminal program. When users log in, they can perform functions, such as uploading and downloading software and data, reading news and bulletins, and exchanging messages with other users through public message boards and sometimes via direct chatting. In the middle to late 1980s, many BBSs offered games that could be downloaded or played against other players.

Cipher: A cryptographic algorithm.

Chargeback: When a cardholder disputes a charge with the bank (the "issuing bank"), the bank may reverse the payment and refund the cardholder after completing an investigation.

Cloud computing: A model for enabling on-demand network access to a shared pool of configurable computing capabilities or resources (e.g., networks, servers, storage, applications, and services) that can be rapidly provisioned and released with minimal management effort or service provider interaction.

Controlled Area Network (CAN): The vehicle bus standard that was designed to allow microcontrollers and devices to communicate with each other in applications without a host computer. CAN was designed as a message-based protocol originally for multiplex electrical wiring within automobiles.

CPU: Central processing unit of a computer.

Critical infrastructure: The systems and assets, whether physical or virtual, so vital to society that the incapacity or destruction of such may have a debilitating impact on the security, economy, public health or safety, environment, or any combination of these matters.

Cryptocurrency: Digital money, such as Bitcoin.

Cryptography: The use of mathematical techniques to provide security services, such as confidentiality, data integrity, entity authentication, and data origin authentication.

Cyber espionage: The practices of obtaining secrets without the permission of the holder of the information. This information is often taken from competitors, rivals, governments, and enemies for economic or personal gain. Typically, cyber espionage (or cyber spying) is accomplished through the use of the internet, proxy servers, malicious software, and hacking techniques.

Cybersecurity: The activity or process, ability, capability, or state whereby information and communications systems and the information contained therein are protected from and/or defended against damage, unauthorized use or modification, and/or exploitation.

Dark Web: The portion of World Wide Web content not indexed by standard search engines that is generally attributed to hacking and illegal cyber activities. Also called the **Deep Web**.

Data breach: The unauthorized movement or disclosure of sensitive information to a party, usually outside the organization, that is not authorized to have or see the information.

Data theft: The deliberate or intentional act of stealing personal and/or sensitive information.

Decipher: To convert enciphered text to plain text by means of a cryptographic system.

Decode: To convert encoded text to plain text by means of a code.

Decrypt: A generic term encompassing decode and decipher.

Department of Homeland Security (DHS): A dedicated group of more than 240,000 employees that secure the nation from various threats. The job disciplines range from aviation, border security, emergency response, and chemical facility inspections to cybersecurity.

Digital Millennium Copyright Act (DMCA): A 1998 United States copyright law that criminalizes the production and dissemination of technology, devices, or services intended to circumvent measures that control access to copyrighted works.

Distributed Denial of Service (DDoS): An attack that prevents or impairs the authorized use of information system resources or services.

Encryption: The process of transforming plain text into cipher text.

Engine Control Units (ECU): Controls a series of actuators on an engine to optimize engine performance. Cyberhackers like to get into the ECU to exploit various sensors.

Federal Communications Commission (FCC): An independent agency of the United States government created by congressional statute to regulate interstate communications by radio, television, wire, satellite, and cable in all fifty states, the District of Columbia, and US territories.

Federal Trade Commission (FTC): An independent agency of the United States government. The principal mission of the FTC is the promotion of consumer protection.

Firewall: A capability to limit network traffic between networks and/or information systems.

Hack: An unauthorized attempt to gain access to an information system.

Hacker: An unauthorized user who attempts to gain or gains access to an information system.

Hacktivist: A computer hacker whose activity is aimed at promoting a social or political cause.

Hashing: A process of applying a mathematical algorithm against a set of data to produce a numeric value (a "hash value") that represents the data.

Honeypot: A computer network or program used to lure in cybercriminals by mimicking likely targets of attack for them.

Incident response plan: A set of predetermined and documented procedures to detect and respond to a cyber incident.

Industrial control system: An information system used to control industrial processes, such as manufacturing, product handling, production, and distribution, or to control infrastructure assets.

Industrial, Scientific, and Medical (ISM): Specific radio bands within the spectrum that are reserved internationally for the use of radio frequency other than telecommunications.

Initial Coin Offering (ICO): Type of funding using cryptocurrencies. A quantity of cryptocurrencies are sold in the form of "tokens" (coins) to investors in exchange for legal tender.

Insider threat: A person or group of people within an organization who poses a potential risk by violating security policies.

Internet of Things (IoT): The networking capability that allows information to be sent to and received from networked objects and devices (such as cameras and smart-home devices/appliances) using the internet.

Internet Service Provider (ISP): An organization that provides services for accessing and using the internet.

Intrusion detection: The process and methods for analyzing information from computer networks and information systems to determine whether a security breach or security violation has occurred.

Intrusion Prevention System (IPS): A network security/threat-prevention technology that examines network traffic flows to detect and prevent vulnerability exploits.

Key: The numerical value used to control cryptographic operations, such as decryption, encryption, signature generation, or signature verification.

Keylogger: Software or hardware that tracks keystrokes and keyboard events, usually surreptitiously/secretly, to monitor actions by the user of an information system.

Light Detection and Ranging (LIDAR): A remote sensing or surveying method that uses light in the form of a pulsed laser to illuminate a target and measure various distances by the reflected light. This technology is used on UAVs and autonomous vehicles, often with 3-D mapping.

Lizard Squad: A black hat hacking group known mainly for its claims of distributed denial of service (DDoS) attacks, primarily to disrupt gaming-related services.

Malicious code: Program code intended to perform an unauthorized function or process that will have an adverse impact on the confidentiality, integrity, or availability of an information system.

Malware: Software that compromises the operation of a system by performing an unauthorized function or process.

Man-in-the-middle (MITM) attack: Using false digital credentials or certificates to fool a device or user into thinking it is communicating directly with the intended site by rerouting internet traffic through another server.

MoneyPak: A stored-value card provided by Green Dot Corp. MoneyPak is typically purchased with cash at a retailer then used to fund prepaid debit cards or online wallet services like PayPal.

National Highway Traffic Safety Administration (NHTSA): Agency of the executive branch of the United States government and part of the Department of Transportation whose objectives are to save lives, prevent injuries, and reduce vehicle-related crashes. The NHTSA is charged with writing and enforcing the Federal Motor Vehicle Safety Standards.

National Institute of Standards and Technology (NIST):
A physical science laboratory that is considered to be a
nonregulatory agency of the US Department of Commerce.
The NIST's mission is to promote innovation and industrial
competitiveness.

National Transportation Safety Board (NTSB):
Independent United States government investigative
agency that is responsible for civil transportation accident
investigation.

Near Field Communication (NFC): A technology that
enables mobile phones and electronic devices to establish
radio communications with each other by bringing them
in close proximity of each other (typically fewer than four
inches). NFC is a short-range wireless communication where
the antenna used is much smaller than the wavelength
of the carrier signal. Although the communication
range of NFC is limited to a few centimeters, NFC alone
does not ensure secure communications because they
are susceptible to relay attacks.

Neighbor Spoofing: A caller-ID spoof strategy that is being
used by phone scammers in an attempt to get victims to
pick up and answer the phone. Thieves specifically modify
the phone numbers that appear with the intent of fooling
those answering when they see a familiar phone exchange,
making them think it is a family member, local business, or
contact in their area.

Null Route: A computer network route that goes nowhere.
Matching packets are dropped and basically ignored rather
than being forwarded, acting as a kind of very limited
firewall.

Onion Routing: A technique for anonymous communication over a computer network in which messages are put in layers of encryption, similar to layers of the vegetable onion.

OS: Operating system.

Password: A string of characters (letters, numbers, and other symbols) used to authenticate an identity or to verify access authorization.

Password Spraying: A type of brute-force attack that cleverly circumvents the lockout functionality by attempting to use only a few of the most common passwords but against multiple user accounts.

Penetration testing: An evaluation methodology whereby assessors search for vulnerabilities and attempt to circumvent the security features of a network and/or information system. Also known as **pen test.**

Phishing: A scam by which an internet user is duped (as by a deceptive email message) into revealing personal or confidential information that the scammer can use illicitly.

Positive Train Control (PTC): An advanced system that was designed to automatically stop a train before it could crash. PTC has been proven effective in preventing train-to-train collisions, as well as derailments that are results of excessive train speed and/or train movements through misaligned track switches.

Privacy: The assurance that the confidentiality of and access to certain information about an entity is protected.

Private key: A cryptographic key that must be kept confidential and is used to enable the operation of an asymmetric (public key) cryptographic algorithm.

Programmable Logic Controllers (PLC): A digital computer used for automation of typically industrial electromechanical processes, such as control of machinery.

Public key: A cryptographic key that may be widely published and is used to enable the operation of an asymmetric (public key) cryptographic algorithm.

Radio Detection and Ranging (RADAR): A radar system that usually operates in the ultrahigh frequency (UHF) or microwave part of the radio frequency (RF) spectrum that is used to detect the position or movement of objects.

Ransomware: A strain of malware that restricts access to a computer that it infects; the hacker demands a ransom to be paid to the originator of the malware (the hacker) in order for the restriction to be removed. The computer data is encrypted until the ransom is paid (usually in Bitcoins) in which a "key" is provided to decrypt the data.

Recovery: The activities after an incident or event to restore essential services and operations in the short and medium term and fully restore all capabilities in the longer term.

RF: Radio frequency.

Risk analysis: The systematic examination of the components and characteristics of various forms of risk.

Rooted: The process of allowing users of smartphones running Android mobile operating system to attain privileged control over Android subsystems.

Rootkit: A set of software tools with administrator-level access privileges installed on an information system and designed to hide the presence of the tools, maintain the access privileges, and conceal the activities conducted by the tools.

Script kiddie: An unskilled individual who uses scripts or programs developed by others to attack computer systems and networks and deface websites.

Secure Sockets Layer (SSL): A secure technology where an encrypted link is established between a browser and a web server. All the data that is passed back and forth between the browser and web server remains private.

Security policy: A rule or set of rules that governs the use of an organization's information and services to a level of acceptable risk, and the means for protecting the organization's information assets.

Sensitive Compartmented Information Facility (SCIF): A US Department of Defense term for a secure room. It can be a secure room or data center that guards against electronic surveillance and suppresses data leakage of sensitive security and military information. Access is normally limited to those with high-level security clearance.

Service Set Identifier (SSID): A sequence of characters that provides a unique name for a Wireless Local Area Network (WLAN). Often the SSID is referred to as a network name.

The purpose of the SSID is so stations can connect to the desired network when there are numerous networks in operation in close proximity.

Short Message Service (SMS): A texting messaging service used on mobile communication devices.

Situational awareness: Comprehending information about the current and developing security posture and risks based on information gathered, observation and analysis, and knowledge or experience.

Social bots: A type of bot that controls a social media account. The social bot spreads rapidly by convincing other users that the social bot is a real person.

Social engineering: An effective tactic that hackers employ to play against human interaction and often involves tricking individuals to break normal security procedures.

SPAM: Undesired or unsolicited electronic messages. These are illegal email messages. The term came from the original SPAM, a canned pork meat product.

Spider: A type of web crawler that is an internet bot and browses the web for the purpose of web indexing.

Spoofing: Faking the sending address of a transmission to gain illegal/unauthorized entry into a secure system.

Spyware: Software that is secretly or surreptitiously installed into an information system without the knowledge of the system user or owner.

Surface web: The portion of the World Wide Web that is readily available to everyone and searchable with standard web search engines, such as Google, Bing, Yahoo, and DuckDuckGo.

Threat: A circumstance or event that has/indicates the potential to exploit vulnerabilities and adversely impact (create adverse consequences for) organizational operations, organizational assets (including information and information systems), individuals, other organizations, or society.

Threat agent: An individual, group, organization, or government that conducts or has the intent to conduct detrimental activities.

Tor (aka The Onion Router): Free software designed to make it possible for users to surf the internet anonymously so their activities and location cannot be discovered by government agencies, corporations, or anyone else.

Trojan horse virus: A type of malware program that is not self-replicating and contains malicious code that, upon execution, carries out actions determined by the nature of the Trojan. Trojans are used to harm computer systems and often cause a loss and/or theft of data.

Two-factor authentication: An extra layer of security known as "multifactor authentication" that requires not only a password and username but also something that only that user has on him or her or has immediate accessibility to, such as a telephone number.

Unmanned Aerial Vehicles (UAV): An aircraft that does not have an onboard human pilot and is often referred to as a "drone."

Ultrahigh Frequency (UHF): Radio frequencies in the frequency range of 300 to 3000 MHz.

Virtual Private Network (VPN): Extends a private network across a public network. This allows users to securely send and receive data across shared or public networks as if their computer were directly connected to the private network.

Virus: A malware program that, when executed, replicates by inserting copies of itself into other computer programs, data files, or the boot sector of the hard drive. Viruses usually perform some type of harmful activity on infected computers, such as stealing hard disk space or CPU time, accessing private information, corrupting data, spamming contacts, logging keystrokes, or even rendering the computer useless.

Vulnerability: A characteristic or specific weakness that renders an organization or asset—such as information or an information system—open to exploitation by a given threat or susceptible to a given hazard.

Wi-Fi: A local area wireless computer networking technology allowing electronic devices to connect using 2.4 GHz and 5 GHz license-free spectrum Industrial Scientific Medical (ISM) bands. Also commonly referred to as WLAN.

White hat: Hackers who use their abilities to identify security weaknesses in systems in a way that will allow the systems' owners to fix the weakness.

Whitelist: A list of entities that are considered trustworthy and are granted access or privileges.

Wi-Fi Protected Access (WPA2): A type of encryption that is used to secure Wi-Fi networks. WPA2 provides unique encryption keys for every wireless client connected to it.

Worm: A stand-alone computer program with the ability to replicate itself and spread to other computers. A worm is spread through a computer network, but it does not need to attach itself to another computer program like a virus does.

Zombie: A computer connected to the internet that has been compromised by a virus, a Trojan horse, or a hacker; it can be for malicious attacks via remote control. DDoS and email spam are both launched from Zombie computers.

Z-Wave: The wireless standard used in smart-home devices. Z-Wave operates in the 800 to 900 MHz radio frequency range and has advantages over Wi-Fi and Bluetooth, which operate in the 2.4 GHz radio spectrum and often contend with interferers. Z-Wave devices link up together to form a mesh network that provides efficient communications by hopping from device to device.

About the Authors

Scott N. Schober is the president and CEO of Berkeley Varitronics Systems (BVS), a forty-seven-year-old family-owned company in New Jersey that designs and builds advanced wireless solutions and products for worldwide telecom and security markets. He is the Chief Media Commentator for Cybersecurity Ventures. He is a cyber-security and wireless technology expert, author, and weekly video podcast host. Scott's first book, *Hacked Again*, is a top-selling cybersecurity book and currently boasts 190 five-star reviews on Amazon. *Hacked Again* chronicles his experiences as a hacking victim when BVS was hacked in 2013 and how he overcame his circumstances and shared his experiences to help others avoid being hacked.

Scott is a highly sought-after cybersecurity expert for media appearances on hundreds of news networks, including Bloomberg TV, *Good Morning America*, NPR, CNN, Fox Business Channel, CGTN, i24 News, News 12 NJ, and many more. Scott also regularly presents on cybersecurity best practices for small business and consumer protections, wireless threat detection, ransomware, and distracted-driving technology for events, including at RSA 2018, FutureCon, SecureWorld, ShowMeCon, Cyber Investing Summit, ERII Counterespionage Conference,

Connected World, IEEE, NJTC, Mobile World Congress, and numerous local small business workshops and webinars. www.ScottSchober.com.

Craig W. Schober is a writer, videographer, and the communications manager of Berkeley Varitronics Systems (BVS). In addition to his contributions to and edits of *Hacked Again*, Craig creates all marketing content for BVS in the form of weekly blogs, white papers, website and e-commerce design and management, video podcasts, and viral video campaigns. Craig works closely with Scott as both a technical writer and video editor and has also worked in the film and video industry for the past twenty-five years, including as the writer, director, editor, and producer of his own award-winning feature films available on iTunes. He also happens to be Scott's younger brother.

They can both be contacted through
www.bvsystems.com.